MW00879895

Dienr (dear)

Breedlove

An Autobiography

.

Christopher L. Breedlove

I hope this book helps my family understand me. I also hope to inspire other people who are or have been adopted to seek their roots. As an adoptee, you have a right to your past. Even if you are scared, seek your truth, and remember the sounds of the truth are rare.

-Christopher L. Breedlove

"Man doesn't learn the most from answers but questions." - Anonymous

The Box

by Ron Leech

The Box sat on our mantelpiece

For all the world to see.

A simple square of wood and glue

That held the truth of me.

My parents told me what it was

When I was barely three.

But to touch it was forbidden,

I was told to let it be.

"If the Box is mine," I asked my mom

When I was eight or so,

"Let me see just what it holds,

I'd really like to know."

She answered me with tear-filled eyes,

In a voice both tense and low.

"To open it," she hissed to me,

"Will only lead to woe."

"Childless were your dad and I,

Until you came along.

Our natural child, you could not be,

But we knew you would belong.

We adopted you to make us whole,

To complete our family's song.

Your past was sealed into the Box,

To break that seal is wrong."

"Your birth mom is a tarnished lass,

A truly careless one.

There was no way for her to cope,

To care for you, my son.

Because of you, on a downward spiral,

Her reputation spun.

There's a lesson to be learned here, lad,

That life's not always fun."

"But she gave you up, so now her life

Continues without strain.

All our lives are altered now,

As if the past were slain.

And you? You're such a special boy,

With everything to gain.

To tamper with that sacred Box

Will only lead to pain."

It was if Pandora's Box itself,

Lay on that mantel's edge.

I believed that if I opened it,

A painful past I'd dredge.

And between the folks who cared for me,

I'd drive a hurtful wedge.

For years I would ignore that Box

Upon the dusty ledge.

Often I would stare at it,

When through the room I'd pass.

As years went by, it seemed to grow,

In size and shape and mass.

One side turned into a pane

Of smoky one-way glass

That offered me a moment's glimpse

Into that dark morass.

Yet I fought the urge to look inside

As years danced swiftly by.

I found less time to ponder on

The who and what and why.

I was so sure I had no right

Into my past to pry.

I just assumed on the mantel top,

My truth would always lie.

My daughter told me late one night

That soon she'd be a bride.

She kissed my cheek and said to me,

"Dad? Tell me what you hide.

The Box can tell us who we are,

Let's take a look inside.

I'd like to know just where we're from,

It's long past time you tried."

By now the box had grown so large,

I knew the time was right

To look inside this ancient hoax

And free me from its blight.

It fell to pieces in my hands,

And much to my delight,

The truth was then revealed to me

Through a bright and joyful light.

The truth was simple and quite healing.

It caused no harm or shame.

My birth mom had been a frightened lass

Of slender size and frame.

To lose me to adoption

Had never been her aim.

But her parents made her give me up,

And play the truth less game.

For the first time, I saw who I was

In my mother's eyes and face.

"I was told that you had died," she sobbed,

"Of you there would be no trace.

Though my parents thought this cruel lie

Would save me from disgrace,

I prayed each day that you were safe

And in a loving place.

"They said without you my life could be

Just like it was before.

That time would heal the broken heart,

The 'temporary' sore.

But tell no one about this

So you'll not be called a whore.

They made me sign some papers,

Then shoved me out the door.

"It's hard to keep a secret

That hurts the very soul.

Instead of feeling better,

I was in a deeper hole.

But I kept you in my heart

As a barely glowing coal.

It gives me life to see you now,

Alive, aware, and whole."

When I told my parents what I'd done,

They were obviously dismayed.

They weren't quite sure just what to say,

They seemed to feel betrayed.

I reassured them of my love

So their fears would be allayed.

But I asked for understanding

In decisions I had made.

But they could not seem to comprehend

The reasons for my quest.

They'd hoped the truth would stay interred

In that damned old wooden chest.

And the fact that I now felt at peace

They just could not digest.

There were no words for me to speak

That would put their fears to rest.

When the Box was filled so long ago,

False assumptions formed a seal.

"If the birth mom gave the child away,

All her pains of loss would heal."

And "An instant family will make the pain

Of infertility much less real."

Or "The child will bear no ill effects

From this closed and secret deal."

Boxes are a legacy

Of the Closed Adoption age.

Some deal with them quite easily,

Some deal with fear and rage.

It's time to open records

And turn another page.

So all members of the Triad

Can be released from this old cage.

To say I need protection from

The past is just not true.

I have a right to know myself,

Like non-adoptees do.

What good are laws that keep my roots

Hidden from my view?

It's time to raise our voices

And write these laws anew.

The Box is gone, the past is free,

But the quest will never end.

Broken hearts and shattered dreams

We somehow need to mend.

Openness and honesty

Are rights we must defend.

To keep us free of Boxes,

Our path must never bend.

Shared with permission from the author.

Adoption Is Adaption by Kendra Silva

The ability to adapt is as natural as breathing to an adoptee. As a baby, the person who gave me life is gone. I adapt. My adoption is a private family matter never to be discussed. I adapt. My class has a genealogy assignment, but I don't know my heritage. I adapt. A medical assistant hands me a family medical history form, but I can't fill it out. I adapt. In the genetic mirror, I see no reflection. Nobody looks or acts like me. I adapt. My family says I am betraying them because I yearn for answers. My family does not adapt. I adapt. The ability to adapt is one superpower of an adoptee. Adoption is Adaption. I am a Warrior of the Adapted, fighting for understanding love. I adapt.

Important Details Before Reading & Character List

To avoid any confusion throughout *Diehr Breedlove*, I refer to my mother and father the Breedlove's (the people who raised me) as "parents." I acknowledge my biological parents by their first names: "Brenda" and "Undrey" or "birth mother" and "birth father."

Throughout the book, I also include Reflection Points and Alternate Perspectives.

The Reflection Points are where I fill in the blanks of questions or things that you didn't know, or I talk about feelings that I had looking back on my life occurrences as well as lessons I have learned through my journey.

Alternative Perspectives are additional points of view (besides my own) about challenges that I have faced in seeking self-discovery and to give insight on how others could have potentially felt about what I said or did to them.

Characters:

Christopher: Mid 20's Biracial social media manager, dogmatic, aggressive, sagacious, intense.

Father: Early 40s Biracial truck driver, secretive, distant, submissive, hard-working, obsequious.

Mother: Early 50s African-American underwriter, and studio owner, workaholic, dominant, outspoken, loyal.

Sister (I was raised with): 20-year-old biracial undergrad student, compassionate, sarcastic, quiet, avoidant.

Birth Father: Late 50s African-American pastor, assertive, macho, influential, remorseful, consistent.

Birth Mother: Late 50s Caucasian plastics engineer, altruist, docile, penitent, resilient.

Durabi: Early 30s Biracial man, technical writer, aloof, intellectual, inconsistent, haughty, stimulating.

Grandmother: Early 70s Caucasian retired, outspoken, loyal, compassionate, empathetic.

DEDICATION

To Mom & Dad

Despite the fact that you don't understand, and you think that I am ungrateful, I still thank you for loving me for all of these years and being those people who NEVER left even through our difficult times. I am so grateful for the existence of both of you, and I love the ground you walk on. Words cannot express the emotional depth of appreciation and loyalty I feel for you. Thank you for adopting me and taking in my sister with me. Thank you for keeping us together.

I love you more than you can comprehend even though you don't understand my quest on unveiling who I am and the importance of knowing and building relationships with my birth parents. Despite it all, I am indebted to you.

CONTENTS

ACKNOWLEDGMENTS

Thank you to the main source of my inspiration and strength, my younger sister. I love you more than any walking being or thing on this earth. Secondly, thank you to the parents who raised me and the parents who created me. I have room in my heart for all of you, and you all deserve acknowledgment.

If I have encountered you at any point in my life, I thank you. However, a special thanks to these people:

Thank you, Raheem Kareem, Bianca Byers, and Monica McLeggon.

Micah Sanders and Anthony Charaman, thank you for over ten years of love and support.

Thank you: Addison Witt, Christopher Webb, Jessie Elliot, Jenny O, Darell Armentrout, Cierra Carter, Jason Bush, Nyobe Miller, Jeshua Miller, Davianna Butler, Ariel Davis, Jewell Bell, Abriel White, Sam Kashew, Katie Golfetto, Michael Bellmore, Daria Rottenberk, Caitlin Wagner, Merna Yas, Jackie Bain, Joey Higgins, Nada Sedki, Aubrey Ventura, Torrey & Troy Talifer, Francesa Wodja, Antheny Raiy, Gary Weisserman, Kyle Heffelbower, Lisa Maddalena, Gayle Sturt, Jenny Lane, Rasheedah Wright, Cliff Stovall

My dog Tiago, who is my world.

ALL of my family. If we are related, I am grateful and give thanks to you, too.

Thank you to every person at my former high school Oakland Early College.

Thank you to my newest siblings and our growing bonds: Undreya, Anthony, Chante', Bren, and Kristyn.

Thank you to my editor: Shonell Bacon
Thank you to all involved with the book cover.

Cover Credit: Photographed by Detroit based creative director Kashira Dowridge.

Production Assistants: Thalia Esparza, Courtney M, Sarah Johnson.

Makeup Artist: Jasmine Jones

Thank you all for being apart of my journey.

Introduction

People say that most of your pain as an adult stems from your childhood. If we don't acknowledge and work through that pain, our lives can spiral out of control.

Without fully understanding or trying to make sense of the past, you never really know yourself. I have noticed that so many people take knowing their roots for granted. When we know our roots, when we are aware of our biological history, we can become more aware of things relating to our health—even our personality traits. It is more difficult to know who you are and why you do the things you do without a direct source to your own biology.

Throughout this book, I will be sharing my experiences of being an adoptee as well as how I dove into seeking self-discovery. In the midst of seeking and liberating myself, I was able to locate and meet my biological parents in less than a week.

I initially sought out my biological parents to help me understand my health, rejection, and abandonment issues.
When I learned that I had syncope, I had a hard time finding information about it and finding relatives who might also have the same ailment. I knew that health issues like this could be hereditary, and in finding my birth parents, I could learn about this and other possible issues that could affect

me.

In speaking of rejection and abandonment, I will reveal something to you: throughout my entire life, I had VERY violent reactions and vengeful behavior whenever relationships ended or people left my life. It got bad, and I knew it wasn't okay to feel or be this way, so I sought to understand why my behavior would go to such extremes. Finding my parents and learning about my life before adoption answered these questions.

Before meeting my birth parents, my life could be seen as a half-filled photo album. When we grow up, we are embarrassed when our parents pull out the children albums for friends and mates to view. My childhood albums started at age 4. No one could ever really explain to me why that was so. And despite the happy pictures in that album, there were snapshots in my mind, pictures of people and situations that didn't fit the life I had. I felt strongly, however, that those snapshots did fit to some photo album of my life that I could not see. Understanding how these snapshots fit into my past would allow me not only to complete my childhood albums, but also to create a new set for my future.

Another wonderful thing about finding my birth parents? It gave me the opportunity to see people who *looked like me*.

This book is not just a cathartic journey. It's also for you. When I found out I was adopted and met my biological parents, I felt like I was two people: Christopher Anthony Diehr (my biological name) and Christopher Lyndon Breedlove (my name).

I felt connected to both parts of these people, and at the same time, both of these people are me. I decided to share my story to inspire other people who are adopted to seek where they come from and to question the answers that they are given.

In order to know who you are, you must know where

you come from.

I hope you walk in faith and courage to know where you come from, too. Lastly, at the end of the book, I decided to share a few different writing pieces that I wrote to poetically express feelings I had regarding certain challenges that I have experienced in my life.

Diehr Breedlove acts as both a collection of letters to myself to chronicle my truth and as confirmation that I own my dual identity.

"There is great power in understanding your past." - Christopher L. Breedlove

PART ONE
Adoption and Abandonment

Hidden Secret

Dear Breedlove,

I remember the day I found out I was adopted almost like it was yesterday.

Growing up, I used to ask my mother whether I was adopted all the time. Her response to my question? Her response came in the form of a question.

"Do you think God makes mistakes?"

I responded, "No."

And she said, "There is your answer."

I always thought that I was adopted, so when my mother confirmed that I was not adopted, I began to tell myself that I was not adopted.

A few years later, my mother and I got into a disagreement. The disagreement was about if I could spend the weekend at my friend Stone's house, and my mother said no. Very rarely did I ask to do much of anything, and I didn't understand why my mother said no.

My grades were good, I wanted to know a better reason than just "no because I said so."

So, lunch hour began to approach, and I was sitting on one of the couches in J building of my high school, and I randomly called my grandmother. My grandmother was one of my favorite people; she always calmed me down, and she understood me emotionally. It was weird.

I called her, and I vented about the disagreement with my mother. I randomly told her that I felt like I was adopted.

And my grandmother said, "You are."

When my grandmother said that, I was stunned and shocked at the same time. I was 17 and just now hearing that I was adopted?

I felt so angry and betrayed. The two people whom I was supposed to trust the most lied to me. I quickly got off the phone with my grandmother and contacted both of my parents.

My mother was very hesitant to discuss anything. It was almost as if she was more concerned with being angry at the fact that I now knew that I was adopted.

My mother would say things, such as "Why is your grandmother being nosey? This is not her business" instead of being concerned with my questions for her. Every question I asked her, she deflected.

The overall story my grandmother and father told me was that my birth mother was an alleged drug addict and left me for a week in an apartment building, Child Protective Services were called, and I was placed into foster care.

Afterwards, I talked to my dad, who was a little more cooperative. He told me my last name before Breedlove was Diehr, pronounced *dear*. My father disclosed all that he knew. One of the main reasons I felt angry about it was because I felt like it was a "typical adoption story." I was upset because I found out my sister was actually my biological sister. I was sad at that because I didn't want her to feel the pain of feeling unwanted or abandoned due to our birth mother abandoning us.

The night I found out I was adopted, I went to a party and got completely trashed so as not to think about what I just learned. I even had memories that nobody could account for. I wondered, *Why was it fair that everyone in the family knew my story, but I didn't even know my own?*

For me, this was the first level of abandonment. I felt excluded. Everyone in my family basically lied to my face for years. I considered withholding information as a form of lying. Even now looking back on things, I understand they were trying to protect my sister and me, but why was it fair for the entire family to know except for us?

Growing up, abandonment issues were something I had always struggled with. I would always ask my parents if they were going to leave me. I would even have difficulty getting over temporary crushes. Any end to a relationship with another person and my feelings would be really hurt. And, when I say my feelings were hurt, I mean butt hurt.

I have always wondered why I was different.

Why was I the shortest in the family?

Why did I have green eyes?

How come nobody really looked like me?

Why don't I have baby pictures?

Why do I only have pictures from 4 years old and up?

These are questions I questioned myself with every day growing up around the age of 14 or 15 and maybe even earlier than that.

I even wondered why I remembered the name Brenda?

Who was she?

Why did I remember this name?

|||||||

Dear Breedlove,

Before I go into detail about my experience in learning of my adoptive past, I want to talk about the different levels of abandonment, first discussing the sense of abandonment from being adopted, how I reacted, and how it led to issues in my relationships."

If you do not do the work or find your roots, you will continue cycles or repeat certain lessons until you fully understand the root of where your issues stem from.

Even after having knowledge that I was adopted, it was still something our family kept private. My parents used to tell me that it wasn't my place to tell my sister. If I told her that she, too, was adopted, I would cause a rift in my relationship with my parents. I even had threats of getting kicked off of my mother's health insurance if I mentioned the adoption to my sister. I didn't understand why everyone was so harsh with throwing the adoption up in my face, but when it came to my sister, people in the family wanted to be so secretive of the matter.

There was a handful of family members that told me I was adopted. I just remained confused why nobody wanted to be this honest with my sister and tell her about her truth. I even remember asking my parents blatantly if they ever intended on telling my sister about her adoptive past.

They said no.

However, I understood this because the adoption was intended to be a "closed adoption." During the last eight years of my life, I have been the "black sheep" of my family because I'm the only one who wants to talk about the truth. I was the only one who was not resisting reality. I wanted the adoption to be talked about and celebrated instead of ignored.

In 2016, I told my sister that she was adopted. For some odd reason, we were having a debate about how many crackheads lived in the metropolitan area. One minute we were having a debate, and the next minute we were disagreeing.

In the midst of our argument, I told my sister, "For me being your only blood, you are really mean to me."

My sister immediately told my mother, "Mom, Chris is talking about that adoption stuff again."

Things then took a left turn, when that was not my intent.

My mother then asked me to leave. That's when I looked over to my sister and said, "How she is handling me should be a clear indication that I am right, and that we are adopted." I thought my mom's behavior was odd because she would constantly threaten to involve the police every time the adoption issue came up, making me believe that she had her own issues regarding her infertility.

My mother kept asking me to leave, or she would call the police. I remember facing my mother directly after minutes of me disclosing the adoptive past with my sister.

I glared at her. "Face your truth about us being adopted and stop lying."

She then responded, "You are adopted. She is not."

The emotions I felt when my mother said that to me were overwhelming. Was she disowning me because of my knowledge and awareness of the adoption? Another thought I had after she said that to me was, "You know damn well that she is my biological sister," but I didn't say that aloud.

Even now when I share the story, I can still feel her hands on my back, pushing me out of her house.

I remember thinking, *You call yourself my mother, but you are lying to both your children.* I was confused why she was telling my sister that she was not adopted and had no issue telling me that I was adopted when we were both actually adopted. This caused friction between me and my sister, putting our relationship at risk. My sister always thought I was trying to get her to "hate our family"; instead, I was just trying to let her know the truth.

Overtime, I became jealous of my mother and sister's relationship. Why was she so protective over my sister and not that protective over me? Or even

little things would make me jealous. The fact that my sister was my mom's phone screen saver for over four years used to bother me so much.

Sometimes, I even found myself wondering if I was the family guinea pig? Why do people feel entitled to tell me that I am adopted, but nobody wants to be honest and upfront with my sister about her adoptive past? I understood that it was a painful subject, but I never understood the whole never having

the intent to tell her? It made me question: if my grandmother didn't tell me I was adopted, would my parents have ever shared my adoptive past with me?

While I had a family, I still felt alone. I never fully felt any form of unconditional love from anyone. I always felt there was love present, but it had conditions, which, in some ways, can be a good thing. What I mean by that is conditions could also be considered boundaries, and it is okay to love others but also consider your boundaries that you set for yourself.

But here, when dealing with my own mother and father, I didn't want boundaries. I knew I was more than a halfway, but I wanted—and deserved—unconditional. On top of that, I struggled with figuring out how to feel about my parents keeping the adoption under wraps. Should I have felt good that they were trying to protect me or upset because I felt like they were hiding the past from my sister and I and continued to disregard my emotions or any time I wanted to address the adoption? I felt if they were able to adopt us, why wait to tell us that

we were adopted? I always thought adoption should be celebrated because it is a blessing and should not be kept a secret.

A few days after the incident of telling my sister, I began receiving phone calls from my aunt and cousins, asking, "Why did you hit your mother and sister?"

I was confused. I had never hit my mother and sister. My mother was always been very dramatic. If things didn't go her way, she would exaggerate situations or scenarios to fit her to be the victim instead of owning up when she was wrong. I was accustomed to this because I too acted the same way.

On the day I got this phone call, I was at my grandmother's house, and my mom came by. I asked her why she was lying to family members saying that I hit her and my sister. It was almost as if she convinced herself that actually happened. My mother began telling my grandmother that I hit her and my sister, and I got angry because she again was being dishonest.

An ultimate sense of abandonment settled in me. I felt like nobody really understood how I felt or was trying to for that matter. History just kept repeating, and we kept having the same disagreements about the same things.

Everyone in my family always thought that I was angry about the adoption. The adoption was never an issue to me; in fact, it was a blessing, and I do acknowledge that. I was more so upset at the fact that people chose to lie blatantly to my face about my sister's and my roots. If my parents and family could have addressed the matter instead of avoiding it and deflecting, I would have been more calm about the situation. I felt like I was the only one going through it and that I was the only one trying to face the reality of what was going on. My entire family was living in a false reality. How can you save others who are living in false realities? I was mostly angry because I felt that I needed my parents to help me understand my past and my life, and they chose not to because it made them uncomfortable.

Yes, being adopted was a blessing, but was it okay for my questions about my past to go unanswered because the two main people who adopted me didn't want to admit it or be open to discussions about it? How was it fair not to discuss something in relation to ME and my life and my past?

Was I allowed to have questions or an alternative view when there were people in my life that had the next steps on answers and where they could be provided?

Growing up, I always had tumultuous relationships with people. Family and friends! Things were never really consistent with anyone. I was always accustomed to getting close to people and then them leaving. However, I had impulsive emotional reactions to situations that involved people whom I deeply cared about. I also had a way of testing people to see how far I could go to see if they loved me unconditionally because I didn't feel deserving of love and because I thought others would abandon me. My abandonment issues had a way of making me feel so low about myself. I felt worthless,

unwanted, and ashamed of who and what I was. Which was why it was crucial for me to solve the mystery of my abandonment and neglect issues.

Reflection Point

I always wanted my parents to be more interactive and engaged in my life. I felt the moment after I found out I was adopted. they lost interest in my life because I questioned my role in their life. I felt misunderstood because I wanted to unveil the roots of where I might have come from. I never understood why people felt ashamed of having or adopting a child. When I was younger, everywhere my sister and I used to go, we would always have an ignorant person say something that was out of context.

I remember walking in the grocery store with my mother, and this man had asked her, "Are these your kids? They are lighter than you."

My mother responded, "Yes, you idiot," and shooed them away.

I even remember a time when I was aware of my adoption, and my mother ran into an old friend. I overheard them talking. The woman asked how long my mother was in labor with my sister and me. My mother told her how many hours for the both of our births. But in my mind, I knew that she was not being honest.

Up until now, I knew that adoption and infertility were things my mother was sensitive about. As my mother reads this book, I want her to know that I don't need biology to define her as my mother. She was there for me for the past 21 years.

None of us are perfect, and we all have different ways of doing things and responding to life events that happen to us, and I love her regardless.

| | | | | | |

Twin Sisters Mystery

Dear Breedlove,

From the ages 4-14, I never really questioned my life until I started realizing that I had green eyes and nobody else in the family had them. I always questioned why I didn't have baby pictures. Growing up, I always thought my sister was the biological child because she had baby pictures, and I didn't.

Roughly six months after disclosing our adoptive past to my sister, she called me and asked to talk for a few minutes. She asked me did she have a twin. This was the first time I had ever heard of a twin. When I heard this from my sister, it made me even more curious to know about my adoption. My sister said that the guards questioned my mother regarding the birth certificate on their cruise, and her birth certificate stated that my sister was a twin. Our mother stated to the guards that the twin had died at birth. My sister and I never fully discussed the "twin matter"; we both just ignored the knowledge of knowing that there was a

twin as a possible sibling to us. This information, however, never really left the back of my mind.

Reflection Point

Keep in mind, I am aware that my sister and I are adopted, and she is not aware of her adoptive past. My adoptive family wanted to keep it private for some reason, and we don't discuss the adoption. Period.

Alternative View

Looking back on things, I understood completely why my parents kept things private for a while. I didn't, however, understand to the fullest extent how my parents could have felt about not being able to produce children themselves. They had never mentioned anything about this to me or my sister, but relatives like to talk about grown folk things in front of children, so piece by piece, I would figure this out. My parents wanted to keep the adoption private for the sake of their happiness and contain the safety of my sister's and my emotions of not feeling unwanted or not loved. Growing up, our parents gave us everything we could ever ask for, and all the trips you could imagine every year. I never wanted or yearned for anything materialistically as a child. The only thing I genuinely wanted was to understand my parents and have them understand me.

There were things that we could have all done differently, and everything happened how divine order wanted things to unfold. I know that my parents are not bad people for this delayed secret, and I'm not a bad person for reacting with anger; we all just had a fear of the unknown. The older I get, I realize that the unknown is exhilarating.

PART TWO
Sexuality

Sex

Dear Breedlove,

To me, sexuality is an interesting subject. I have always been intrigued by sex and sexuality in general. As a teenager, I really struggled with my sexuality. Around the same time I found out that I was adopted, I was also having difficulty expressing and owning my own sexuality.

I have always felt like an odd ball or something or someone that was different. Some people may view my sexual preference as wrong, but in my eyes, sexuality does not exist. An analogy that I use to express my view on sexuality is: think about the conveyor belt at the grocery store and a variation of male and female bodies.

Basically, one way I interpret sexuality is that we are personalities inserted into bodies, and our bodies are carriers for our spirits to maneuver around on earth. If you're male, we didn't ask to be males, and
women didn't ask to be women. So why limit love based off the physical appearance of your spiritual carrier?

Growing up, I remember hanging around a family friend named Josh, who I used to do everything with. We used to be interested in the same things. During my puberty stages, I remember him making sexual advances toward me, and these advances were unwanted. I want to say I was roughly about 13, and he was around the same age, but he was taller and bigger than I was. Imagine someone who you don't want to be sexually involved with making sexual advances toward you. I felt embarrassed and ashamed. Even though my body was responding as if I did want to engage, my mind and restraint were saying otherwise.

I remember the disgusting musk scent afterwards, too. I had on my favorite red Hanes underwear. I threw them away because they reminded me of Josh. This experience would lead me to a lot of different, confusing situations throughout my high school and college years.

In hindsight, my high school years were the most difficult for me. I felt as if everyone misunderstood who I was. I was tired of hiding who I was; I just wanted to *be*. I confided in several friends about my sexuality, and the next day, a clear majority of people found out. I was embarrassed.

I even remember one of the people that outed me. My friend at the time, Harris.

In front of the entire class, Harris said, "Christopher Breedlove is dating Henry." The irony of Harris outing me was that years later he stayed in my messages trying to talk to me. I felt angry because people classified me as one thing, but I felt another. I received backlash at home and at school about my sexuality. Yes, I liked men, but I also liked women. I was overwhelmed by other people trying to categorize me. This then effected how I interacted with other LGBT people. I remember condemning them because I was insecure with myself. I felt as if I had to choose a sexuality due to people's thoughts of who and what I was. I felt physically attracted to men and women, but I allowed other people to box me into what they thought I should be.

Regarding my home life and my sexuality, I first shared

my sexuality with my parents at the age of 16. I remember my parents' reactions vividly. At first, they said they always knew, then my mother cried. She said she was crying because it was already difficult being black in life, but to like men and be black? It was like a double offense.

My father's reaction was more silent. Even to this day, he never really expressed his feelings about the situation although his actions, become distant with me, showed how uncomfortable he was. My sexuality was a clear problem with my family's religion.

don't bring any fairies into my home
go to church to get the demon out of you
you're family but you're not family

People may not remember things said, but I have the memory of an elephant and remember what was said and how it made me feel.

For the first few years of my parents' awareness of my sexual fluidity, they remained unsatisfied by it. I remember the second guy that I really liked. His name was Henry. Back when digital cameras used to be a thing, we used to trade cameras and take selfies on them and trade back, nothing inappropriate. One day, my mother ended up finding Henry's camera and asked where mine was.

After she found this, I remember my parents going through my phone to see who was I talking to at the time; I thought I was slick, so I would change guys' names to girl names in my phone so that my parents didn't know what my interest was. This particular time, it didn't work. I remember my mother calling Henry's mother to arrange a day to return the cameras, and afterwards, my mother told me to leave Henry alone.

Looking back on it, my parents were right about Henry;

he was an asshole. But at the time, I felt like my own parents were discriminating against me. Very seldom could I have sleep overs with any of my male friends because of my sexual fluidity. I never understood that growing up. Just because I was attracted to some men didn't mean I was attracted to every male I saw, and the same applied with women. After the incident with Henry and the quick spread of everyone hearing about my sexuality in high school, I remember hating going to high school—until my junior year when I transferred schools.

I've always thought that people doubted my abilities because of my sexuality. I noticed the uncomfortableness by other males in my family when around me due to my sexuality. I remember my mother saying to me, "Even though I disagree with your sexuality, your sexuality does not define you."

Even to this day, those words of advice are some words that I carry with me. Just because I identify with being attracted to both sexes does not mean that is all of who I am or all that I can be.

To me, sex and sexuality are parts of who I am. Society or social norms should not tell us who or what we are nor what or who we should desire sexually. Sexuality is something deeper than what we can consume. Sex is exchanging and emerging yourself into another person spiritually. We don't learn lessons with sex until heartache comes in.

I never understood why sexuality meant so much to other people.

How does someone else's sexual choice or any choice have any effect or control on your life?

I find beauty in everyone, both men and women.
And I was fine with that.

PART THREE
Substance Abuse and Self-Mutilation

Running from Me

Dear Breedlove,

Around the age of 17 after I found out about my adoptive past, I began experimenting with many different drugs. I did things that could have taken my life. One time, I took an entire box of sixteen Coricidin pills, as well as high experimentation with benzos. I practically used a drug every day to get me high. Vicodin, Xanax, you name it, I had it. I even remember experimenting with a horse tranquilizer called Ketamine a few times. In retrospect, it's crazy to think that I experimented with so many things without fully understanding that I could have killed myself with the wrong amount. I wanted to run away from myself so bad. When I was sober, my mind just raced with questions, and when I remained high, I was able to disregard the truth of my adoptive past.

Despite the fact I was happy about the adoption, I felt like I was facing an identity crisis, especially finding out so late in my life in addition to my other issues.

| | | | | | |

BCA

Dear Breedlove,

As I look back, I recall having so many different thoughts. Thoughts on my sexuality and its conflict with religion. Thoughts of feeling unwanted even though I had a family, and feelings of rejection. I had so many overwhelming feelings. Around the age of 16, I felt alone in everything that I was going through, and I wanted an emotional release from the pain that I was feeling on the inside. I walked down to the kitchen, grabbed a steak knife, went back to my room, and began making cuts on different parts of my body. I bled everywhere, and I started crying and banging my head on the ground repeatedly. I had the most chaotic emotional breakdown. I was in so much pain I couldn't feel the physical pain that I was inflicting on myself.

My parents heard me crying and came to my room and took me to the hospital. I remember telling the doctor that my intentions were to harm myself. I had an assessment with a doctor, and she thought that it would be best if I went to a mental hospital. I actually didn't have much of a choice; I HAD to go to this mental institution. I was escorted by paramedics to a place called BCA. I was strapped in a patient chair and in the back of an ambulance to the institution. It was really quiet when entering. I remember arriving pretty late to the mental institution, so everybody was sleeping. When I first arrived, I went into this room, and there were two people: a security guy and a nurse. The security guy bagged all of my clothing and items that I came into the hospital with, including my cell phone, ID, and personal items. The nurse told me to shower and gave me a bag of toiletries and a pair of sweatpants and a sweater.

I showered, and they then gave me some food to eat. After I ate, the nurse escorted me to my bed. I shared a room with a roommate who was sleeping. I remember the beds being extremely uncomfortable; they reminded me of hard cots. I hated it there.

A man woke everyone up, saying, "Wake up, vitals and breakfast in 15 minutes" every day. Time was not your own. They controlled when you ate, when snacks were dispersed, as well as television time. I was there for a matter of days, and I felt like I was in prison. You even had to ask to go to the bathroom.

While I was at BCA, I remember thinking that I knew I needed help, but there were people who were a lot more mentally unstable than I was. I also thought why would anyone send sad people to a place where there is no love present?

Why send people who are depressed to a place where they feel ever more isolated and misunderstood?

The first assessment with a psychiatrist I could never forget. In the assessment, I remember him telling me that I was bipolar and depressed. He began a treatment plan and prescribed me an antidepressant, a mood stabilizer, anxiety relief, and sleeping aid medications. There were a few improvements at my stay at BCA. My parents and grandparents came and visited me, and I felt even more pressed to leave.

After almost ten days in the mental hospital away from my things and family and no music, the first thing I did was grab my headphones and iPod and listen to "Lovers Who Uncover" by Crystal Castles. It was one of my favorite songs at the time. The day I was discharged from the hospital, my parents got me new clothes and new things. I felt so confused as to why they were giving me new things after my meltdowns.

| | | | | | | |

Kingswood

Dear Breedlove,

Two months after being released from the institution, and a few weeks into my treatment plan, I remember feeling like the medication was making me feel even more depressed. I would question whether I should stop taking the medication.

I used one of my medications to get high on. I had a second suicidal incident, I remember talking to the high school counselor Ms. Owlette about all the pressures I was feeling. Before my session with her, I took a handful of the mood stabilizers and the pill that I could get high on. At a certain point, I was non-responsive, and the paramedics were called at my high school, and I was transported to a hospital.

I was in the back of the ambulance for the second time, and I already knew where I was going. Another mental institution; I was right. Another doctor then interviewed me, and he stated that I was suicidal, and I was then transported to Kingwood Mental Institution. When I arrived, the same procedures as the first institution applied. They took all of my clothes and personal belongings and escorted me to my room. Per usual.

I didn't recall this institution being as serious as the one I was in before. I even made a few friends at my stay at this hospital. There, we participated in many recreational activities that were calming, and the group exercises were therapeutic. During my second assessment with a different psychiatrist, they stated that I was bipolar, and he took me off of the antidepressants and put me on a different mood stabilizer. I felt relieved because the antidepressants were dulling my mood. The doctor took me off of the pill that I was abusing, too; I was salty about that.

After about seven days, I was discharged from the second mental institution. I remember feeling so excited to go home and eat normal food because I was tired of eating processed food in the mental hospital. My parents remained hopeful that I would get better mentally; they didn't really show too much of a reaction during my encounters in being institutionalized. If anything, they seemed fearful of my volatile behavior.

Provoking Dad

Dear Breedlove,

Within a week of my release from the second mental institution, I became upset at my parents for going through my things and finding paraphernalia in my book bag. I was pissed because they confiscated a pipe that was given to me by a dear friend for my birthday. I was so angry and irritated about that and not being able to get high, so I chose to provoke my father. I don't even remember the exact reason as to why I was determined to get a rise out of him. On this day, my dad had asked me to stay home because he was going somewhere, and I wanted to go, too. So, I blocked the driveway.

As my dad was trying to leave, he kept asking me to move from the driveway. Instead of moving, I jumped on the back of my dad's trunk and sat on the back of his car and dared him to move.

Mind you, my father and I were in the middle of the street right outside our house with two neighbors that were trying to diffuse the situation. I remember my dad getting out of the car and yelling at me. I felt threatened by him, so I head butted him. I couldn't believe my head didn't hurt after I did that; I was enraged with adrenaline. After that, my father withdrew, and I walked away with the neighbors. Apart of my anger was still from my parents not addressing anything relating to the adoption. I began to suppress my feelings because they were not being regarded.

Shortly after, the doorbell rang at the neighbor's house. It was the police arresting me for domestic violence with my father. I felt mad as hell that my dad just called the police on me. Even though I was irate and out of line, I didn't think that was necessary.

Between you and me, he should have beat my ass.

Being arrested made me feel even more disconnected from my family. Even though I was hurting, people were so quick to get rid of me. I was so terrified in the back of the police car. I remember the handcuffs being cold, and they kept rubbing up against my wrist. I was placed in a holding cell with other criminals for over 13 hours. There were at least 10 people in one holding cell with one bathroom. I used a long sheet of paper towel as a blanket. I even remember the soggy ass egg sandwich that they provided.

The next day, I made bail and was given a court date. The judge had decided for me to complete probation successfully and pass JAMS drug testing and pay court fees and take a 12-week anger management course.

When I completed all the regulations the judge had given me, my record was then cleared. After things calmed down, the dynamic of my family changed, and I felt it. There was a lot of tension and detachment on both ends.

| | | | | | |

Overdose

Dear Breedlove,

After this episode, entirely brought on by myself, I remember feeling even more depressed. I began questioning how I was going to afford to pay the court. At the time, I didn't know how to drive, nor did I have a driver's license. I was working a minimum wage retail job. Every shift I had I would take a bus and walk a mile and a half both ways just to get to and from work.

After a few weeks, things calmed down a little in my home life. Around early spring, I scheduled a college visit because the next year I was going to be preparing to go to college. I spent the night at my grandmother's house because she said she wanted to go to the college visit with me. My grandmother had always been very loyal to me; I loved her endless amounts of food as well as her company.

It was a late evening when I spent the night at my grandmother's house, and I raided my grandparents' cabinets for drugs and found oxycodone from my grandfather's surgery. I don't recall how many I took, but I took quite a few. I felt very nostalgic; I was so high I couldn't stop itching my body.

Beep Beep Beep….

My alarm went off at 6 a.m. sharp to start getting ready for the college visit. I felt like a noodle. I could barely function. I began brushing my teeth, and next thing I knew, my head was in the sink. I tried to brush it off and keep going, and it happened again. I then collapsed and hit my face on the floor. With all the noise I made, I ended up waking my grandmother; the whole point of getting up early was to let her get some extra rest.

My grandmother asked if I was okay and I said, "Yes."

I got back up and collapsed in front of her for the third time. My grandmother then asked me to have a seat while she made some food for me to eat.

Growing up, I always had random fainting spells and thought they were from a lack of sleep. I even had heart scans done and still the doctors couldn't find out where the fainting spells were coming from and what the causes were.

Grandmother asked me if I had taken any drugs, and I lied to her and said no.

She asked me why my body was responding weird and I blamed it on muscle supplements because I was working out a lot. She then called the ambulance, and I was escorted to the hospital, and tests were ran on me. One of the doctors had said that my potassium levels were significantly low, and I had a low-functioning heart rate. I was close to overdosing on codeine and had my system flushed out because of it.

I had to drink liquid potassium, which tasted like metal in a bag; it was disgusting. I asked the doctors not to disclose the actual reason as to why I was in the hospital because I knew I was at the age where I didn't have to share why I was sent into the emergency room. I wanted to keep my drug problem under wraps and private from my family.

| | | | | | | |

Admitting Addiction

Dear Breedlove,

Shortly after my release from the hospital from overdosing, I told the truth.

I remember it was on a Thursday. The day was pretty groggy and gray. I felt an overflow of emotions. On this day, I was in the car with my mother, and out of nowhere, I abruptly said, "Mom, I have a drug addiction."

It felt so freeing to have told my mother that I had a problem with drugs.

She asked me a series of questions, such as:

Have you stolen from me before?

What kind of drugs are you using?"

She even said that she knew I was off, and something was wrong with me, and she kept reiterating that she loved me. The following week, my mother enrolled me in outpatient rehab.

My mother came with me to my first few appointments. I remember hating it. I was in outpatient rehab for roughly four months. It was some people in the rehab that were doing harsher drugs than I was doing. It really did something seeing what other people were like on harder stuff. I almost thought some of the people were crazy in there. For a while, I felt as if the rehabilitation wasn't even working.

But there was a day that changed my mind completely on all drugs except for weed because weed is NOT a drug.

We were sitting in rehab, and they played a documentary on babies who were born with drug addictions. I remember sobbing as soon as I saw that. It made me think about what kind of example I was setting for my sister. I didn't want her to think of me as a not shit brother, and I didn't want to be a product of where I came from. I didn't want to be what my biological mother was, a drug addict. I wanted to be different.

For me, that was the turning point to really try to make changes to myself. I wanted to make a conscious effort to understand myself and seek my roots for myself as well as my sister. In the midst of handling my drug addiction, I kept my sister as the primary source of my motivation. I wanted to be great for her and me. I wanted to be put together so whenever she was broken, I could be her rock.

Reflection Point

People who struggle with drugs and depression have to want to overcome those challenges themselves. It all begins with admitting and talking about the struggles before the struggles actually get better. You can't force a person to want to get over the challenges that were given to them in their life. It is important to be around people who support you and elevate you and even if you don't have that, you have yourself.

PART FOUR
Relationships, Distance, Projection, and Accountability

Durabi

Dear Breedlove,

I have always been a person who was pro relationships. Very rare did I even have feelings for others. For almost five and half years, on and off, I dated a guy named Durabi. He was cool, seductive, educated, and intelligent. He was a former escort, and as he would say, "I'm from Inkster." Looking back on this relationship, I refer to Durabi as my biggest teacher and best friend. Nobody could ever understand the bond that I had with him. He taught me so much about myself and was the one person to push me to seek my roots. We originally met at a local bar (mind you I rarely go out). It was my third time at this particular bar where I met Durabi. We saw each other briefly and went about our separate ways.

From that moment forward, I remember thinking about him obsessively. Six days later, on a Sunday, I stepped out to help my mother with the groceries, and on my phone was his friend request on Facebook along with a message. I was ecstatic! We made plans to go to a drive-in movie and saw *The*

Haunting of Connecticut. I was so drawn to Durabi even past how hot I thought he was. I remember enjoying myself, but my mind would not shut up.

My mind kept repeating "HIV, HIV, HIV." I felt so confused as to why. Almost an hour into the movie, Durabi asked could he share something with me. Of course, I said yes.

"I'm HIV positive," he said, "and I am undetectable and on treatment."

I was in shock because my intuition was saying "HIV," and he actually was HIV positive. I felt honored that he shared his status with me on the first date. I still had interest in him.

"Are you going to run out of the car yet?" he asked. "Are you going to hit me?"

"No."

I felt so bad that people had actually hurt him and said hurtful things to him because of his status. In my eyes, I wanted to put myself in his shoes; I wanted to understand him.

I questioned myself, thinking, *If I had what he had, would I want somebody to love me despite the fact I had a disease?*

Of course, so I decided to pursue Durabi, and I accepted him and didn't care about his status. In the beginning of our relationship, he always made sure I was comfortable talking about it, and he answered any unanswered questions.

Some people called me crazy, but I just saw more to him than how beautiful he was. I saw potential in him very quickly.

What caught me about Durabi was how infectious his energy was and how he was so full of life. I felt as if he was the light, and I was the moth drawn to the light. I remember having a very aggressive attraction toward Durabi. Our conversations would last for hours; I would talk to him between all of my breaks and any chance that I could.

Prior to beginning my relationship with Durabi, he was with a "sugar daddy," and I basically stole him away from the sugar daddy "allegedly." Almost four months into my relationship with Durabi, he moved and got a job in Georgia while I remained at University in Michigan.

Even with the distance, Durabi and I tried to make our relationship work. We communicated literally all day for at least six to eight hours, no exaggeration. Durabi and I were morbidly obsessed with each other. After a while, we began fighting over missed phone calls on both ends (we were both pretty possessive in the beginning). We even wrote letters to each other to express ourselves. As the relationship continued to unfold, I recall Durabi and I trying to change each other instead of accepting each other, which led to A LOT of fighting.

We both had HIGH insecurities about what the other was doing to the point we were both trying to control each other. He would tell me what I could and could not do or where I could and could not go or vice versa.

We mirrored each other, we had similar childhood experiences, father relationships and addictions. I remember always referencing Durabi as my spiritual mirror.

During arguments, Durabi would take the past struggles that I confided in him about and use them as weaknesses.

"At least I know who my mother is, who is your mom?"

"Your mom is a bitch."

"Your parents should have returned you to the dumpster where they found you."

After hearing all of those jabs, I felt so angry with the things Durabi would say to me when we would have disagreements about our relationship. I started getting even with him, saying things like:

"At least I don't have HIV."

I felt…

"If you wanna take it there, we can take it there."

I never have been the type of person to harm a person with their own secrets. In a way, I was appalled because he was almost seven years older than me acting as if he was my age or younger. We lacked problem solving in our relationship and simple communication. We had an unhealthy way of pushing each other's buttons. And there were already additional stressors in the relationship due to the distance strain.

Looking back on it, Durabi and I ignored all of the problems that we had in our relationship. The relationship involved an intense physical, spiritual, emotional, and intellectual attraction to one another. We had a lot of things we needed to work on in learning to accept each other. It's like we both knew we were no good for each other in those moments, but we stayed together even though we knew on a spiritual level that we loved differently. In those moments, I realized that we both had hurt from our past that we needed to solve. I had to solve my abandonment issues because he would often say I would project those on to him. And Durabi had to overcome his issues regarding his HIV status and not feeling good enough.

Durabi was the only person I felt that really understood and connected with me and knew who I actually was. For a Christmas gift, he got me an ancestry.com DNA kit because I was always curious to know what my heritage was.

I even remember a time I visited him in 2014, and we cried together on New Year's. We agreed that our relationship was to teach each other how to love ourselves, but we ignored the red flags and needed to learn to communicate and problem solve better in order to keep our relationship going; we also needed some space.

Reflection Point

In retrospection, a lot of people used to judge me for my choice of relationships. Especially my family. I understood that they were concerned about me, but I wasn't. I think nowadays there are so many negative stigmas regarding HIV. For the longest, it took me awhile to understand Durabi's struggle with HIV until the stigmas started happening to me. Some people knew I was involved with a positive partner and would tell me that they were scared to
engage with me. In those moments, it helped me understand the negative stigmas Durabi was talking about, and I understood his pain.

People with HIV and all other illnesses deserve love, too. People need to take the proper time to educate themselves instead of verbally expressing ignorance. If you were in their shoes, I'm sure you would want someone to love you unconditionally past your illness, too, wouldn't you? If you are a person who is positive or dealing with a disease, know that you are worth it and worth someone loving you unconditionally.

To this day, I still love Durabi unconditionally. I don't want to harp on the relationship piece too much because my book is mostly about self-discovery, but Durabi was my greatest teacher; he brought awareness to my abandonment issues and how I projected them onto him and others in my relationships. I had a difficult time managing and maintaining close relationships with other people, including him.

After my rocky relationship with Durabi ended, I made a choice that relationships with other men were not for me. I felt traumatized, and I always felt like something was missing in my previous encounters.

Any-who, I am now learning to control that energy because it is not the responsibility of another person. I think a lot of times we get involved in relationships looking for a person to "fix" us, or we expect them to make us feel a certain way, but in all actuality, that is not their issue. It is up to us to solve our own issues that we internally deal with and personally deal with insecurities instead of deflecting that pressure onto the other person involved in the relationship.

A lot of times, we encounter situations or people that make past traumas or internal issues come out, and that's exactly what happened with me. For years, I struggled with abandonment issues that stemmed from being left by my biological mother. It constantly came out when people left my life whether it be a friend or a crush, etc. I believe in the importance of understanding trigger points that change your behavior because if you are mindful of what triggers certain emotions, you are able to gain more control over yourself. Which is why I think understanding your past is so crucial. Most people confuse "living in the past" and "understanding the past." The two are completely different. Living in the past is having the inability to move forward in relationships in a new way or constantly blaming others for actions done in the past. However, understanding the past is being mindful of what happened in the past, in an effort to control or prevent certain actions from occurring in your present or future. Without understanding problems or issues you face from the past, how can you have a successful future? It is not up to other people to solve your life mystery; it is up to you.

The experience with Durabi also showed me that we all have toxic traits, and it is our duty to make ourselves aware of the toxicity that we may bring to a relationship.

Savannah Coast
Dear Breedlove,

A few years into my distant relationship with Durabi, I

decided to drive 36 hours from LA to GA to try to make things work with Durabi, seeing as we were in an on-again, off-again relationship for five and a half years. Roughly four days in, I had another self-harming incident, and I was taken to the hospital by Durabi. Prior to being exported to the hospital, Durabi and I were in a heated disagreement about loyalty, and it escalated. For some reason, that disagreement made my abandonment issues surface, and I began punching myself in the face full force and ran to the kitchen and slit my arm. I was so accustomed to taking pain out on myself instead of finding productive ways to manage my pain. The thought of losing my relationship with Durabi killed me inside, and I didn't really know myself outside of that relationship with him, nor did I know who I was or what I even wanted.

In the hospital, I remember going crazy. It was my third time being institutionalized. The fact that I basically was dumped after driving 36 hours to make a relationship work, I was livid. I remember throwing notebooks, binders, and whatever was in sight because I was so damaged. I then began to calm myself down.

About 15 minutes went by, an advisor approached me with a needle and said that I needed a shot to calm me down. It was apparent that I was calmer, and I told her that I didn't need a shot to calm me down and that I was fine. The advisor then tried to force the needle in me after I said I didn't need it.

I grabbed her arm and took the needle and threw it.
She then walked away and came back with six men who took me into a room with no windows and pinned me in the corner, pulled my pants down, and gave me a shot in my butt. After, they locked me in that room for a few hours.

While I was in the hospital, I was diagnosed with borderline personality disorder. I shared the supposed mental condition with Durabi, and he said that he did not want to date any person with a mental disease. Funny part of that statement was I was having unprotected sex with a person who had a physical disease that had a stigma of being life-threatening—but I wasn't complaining. I was accepting of him and his condition, but he fled in my time of need.

During my final visit with the head doctor, he stated that it took six to nine months to diagnose a person with borderline personality disorder. He also said that I was not mentally unstable and that I was in love with a person who did not love me. The doctor

The day before I was discharged from the mental hospital, Durabi brought my car, packed with all of my belongings, to the hospital.

The day I was discharged from the hospital, I could not contain myself. On the inside of my car was a letter from Durabi stating, "You will understand later, and I'm sorry."

I felt so angry I threw away my whole life for him. A week prior, I drove over 36 hours, and now I had to drive 18 hours back home with a broken heart? Luckily, my grandmother flew down to Georgia to drive with me back home. If she wasn't there with me, I don't know what I would have done.

Reflection Point

In my relationship with Durabi, I was accepting of consistent ups and downs because it was all I knew. I thought being disrespected, ignored, and pitied were a part of having a relationship. However, my volatile behavior didn't make things any easier for me to better my relationship with Durabi. An additional lesson I learned from this relationship and my home life is that I still had issues that resonated from my home life and childhood that needed to be resolved because they were being displayed in my personal relationships, and I knew that if I did not work on them, they would repeat in different relationships.

Alternative Perspective

In Durabi's view, I understood why he removed me from his home and sent me packing. He never experienced anybody inflicting harm on themselves. Perhaps in those moments, Durabi was overwhelmed and felt pressured or questioned who I was when he saw those parts of me in my responses. In his defense, perhaps he didn't feel it was his responsibility to heal me, and I needed to go home to work on solutions on healing myself.

Reflection Point II

If we don't attempt to solve our childhood problems, they are just extra baggage. I even think to this day that "Sometimes when we as people cannot separate from things or people that are not right for us at the right time, things must happen for us to understand God or the Universe must interfere to remove us from the relationship to reflect on ourselves."

PART FIVE
My Adoption Paperwork and the Truth

Entering Self-Discovery

Self-discovery is the ultimate form of discovering yourself as well as your purpose. Becoming more self-aware is necessary to transform into the person you are meant to become.

Growing up, I didn't have any of the answers, and nobody wanted to provide them to me, so I sought them for myself. After years of not knowing what happened to me for three years of my life, I now could chronologically assess my life, and it felt good to have done the work to get the answers I needed to heal my overall issues with abandonment and rejection.

"How much better to get wisdom than gold, to choose understanding rather than silver." Proverbs 16:16

The Letter

Dear Breedlove,

The only leads that I had to finding information from my adoption was a few websites that my previous partner Durabi gave me. I never fully exhausted the tools because I was afraid of discovering my roots. I had a conversation with Durabi, and he had said, "How can you want to help others and talk about your adoption story when you didn't even try to look for where you came from?"

At the time, I thought that comment was so disrespectful, but as the months went on, I realized that he was right.

On Monday, September 26, 2016, I chose to write a letter to the Central Adoption Registry, requesting information about my adoption. The adoption was closed, and my birth mother had terminated her rights as a parent because she was a cocaine addict and could not be found.

Below is the letter I sent to the adoption registry.

Hello,

My name is Christopher L. Breedlove, and I am seeking additional information about my closed adoption, adoption records, and original birth certificate. Below is all of the information I know and enclosed is a copy of my photo ID and date of birth.
I was born in Troy, MI (Oakland County).
The story of my adoption from what I know as of 9/26/2016:

My biological mother was a drug addict. She left me in an abandoned apartment building. I was found by CPS and put into Foster Care. The adoption center was called: Evergreen Child Services. Roughly four years later, I was adopted by my adoptive parents. My adoptive parents received additional information of a second child shortly after I was adopted, and it was a set of twins (boy and girl). The male twin died, and the sister twin who lived was adopted by the same family as I was.

I look forward to any information given.

Best,

Christopher L. Breedlove

| | | | | | |

Microfilm

Dear Breedlove,

On October 22, 2016, I received a letter from the Department of Human Services stating that they found my adoption records, and they were on microfilm. It would take roughly twelve weeks to process the files. This letter made me excited and scared at the same time. I remember feeling happy to receive the letter. But for some reason, I also felt ashamed to even seek the adoption papers. I felt a lack of loyalty to my adoptive parents. I didn't want them to feel upset or angry about my choice to pursue the truth regarding my birth family. I didn't want my parents to feel less than a man or woman or a parent. I wanted them to know that I loved them, and whatever information I found would only help me understand myself.

The day I received information on my adoption file being located, I visited my mother to check and see if the mail had arrived.

As soon as I entered the house, she said, "I know you are trying to find those people."

Why are you going through my mail was what I really wanted to say, but I didn't.

"You are *my* son," my mother said. "What your birth mother did, a mother does not do and that is leave their child."

I started tearing up because I knew how much my mother loved me, and I loved her the same in return despite our tumultuous relationship.

To show my parents and other loved ones respect, I decided to keep quiet for a few months about any pursuits of information on my adoption because I didn't want any drama. I didn't want family members disliking me for having a curiosity to seek where I came from. I didn't want people in my family feeling bad or taken for granted.

| | | | | | | |

100+ Pages

Dear Breedlove,

My adoption papers came in the mail March 27, 2017. It was a 100-page packet. It had social worker reports, birth information, intelligence test, foster family notations, and information on who my biological parents were. There was so much information. After years of not being able to chronologically assess my own life, I now had the information to do so.

It was overwhelming.

In the papers, it stated that I was born April 29 at 10:26 p.m. My height and weight were not done at the hospital prior to transfer. I was born prematurely and was only three pounds. My APGAR scores were 3 and 7. After developing respiratory distress, I was intubated and transferred to a nearby hospital's intensive care nursery. I remained at the ICU for two months until I was able to be released to my birth mother. I was born to Brenda Diehr (pronounced like *deer*), and Stephen Diehr was listed as my biological father. Another man named Undrey Dean was also listed as a putative father. I was named Christopher Anthony Diehr. My biological mother was allegedly a cocaine addict. For over a week, she left me with some neighbors in her apartment complex. She got so high she forgot about me and didn't come back.

The adoption services supposedly tried to locate the whereabouts of both of the men who were considered my biological father but were unsuccessful. They tried contacting them via mobile and at the addresses provided. Both men were nowhere to be found.

The records also stated that there was a case worker who testified against my birth mother, stating that she was married in Oakland County in 1979 and that there was no record of a divorce. The rights of her husband and alleged father "Stephen Diehr" were terminated. The rights of putative father Undrey and the biological mother Brenda were terminated, too. After my birth parents' rights were terminated, I was placed into the foster care system. After further reading of the document, I learned that my biological mother was incarcerated.

Prior to being adopted by my current family the Breedlove's, I was placed into one foster care home. The papers didn't have much detail about my first placement.

However, in the first foster home, it was noted that I was physically abused and neglected.

The intelligence reports indicated that at the age of 3, my IQ level was below a 77, which is very low. I was not potty trained, nor did I know how to put on my own clothes. It even stated that there were periods as long as six days that I would go without saying much of anything.

Social worker reports stated that I was a shy child and interacted well with other children. However, I also experienced emotional deprivation. I learned that I used to sleep walk and that synced with syncope, a current issue I have been dealing with for a few years.

In the midst of being adopted by my adoptive family, social worker reports stated there was a clear bond with my adoptive parents, and they heard me laugh for the first time when meeting the Breedlove's. I even called them Mom and Dad.

After being adopted by the Breedlove's, there were drastic improvements. I was potty trained and knew how to put on my clothes after a few short months with my parents. I was also enrolled in speech development classes and special education classes to get me on board with other children my age educational wise. My adoptive parents worked with me a lot due to the neglect I suffered in my previous foster care home.

From an emotional standpoint, the social worker said that I enjoyed playing with children and could be perceived as shy, and at times, I seemed sad or depressed. The social worker also indicated that I was very careful about closeness and being intimate with other people. It was indicated that I was under socialized, and it was difficult for me to bond and form attachments to other people.

After reading some of this information for the first time, I was overwhelmed because memories of names that I remembered resurfaced. The one name I had known my entire life, Brenda, was that of my birth mother's.

Reflection Point

I was not aware of any of this information until I first received my adoption papers March 27, 2017. Below, I provide you the reader with even more information that I learned.

According to the papers, I was removed from my first foster care home due to living conditions and physical abuse.

The only memory I have prior to being adopted is this old lady with a bob style hair cut who always cooked in the kitchen. I also remember two men who would always argue (one guy wore an apple hat with a gap in between his teeth). I shared a bed with a white woman and a black man. I even remember myself sitting in a corner coloring and a lady coming over and kneeling down in front of me and blowing cigarette smoke in my face. And that day just so happened to be the day that my parents saved my life.

I began the adoption process with my mother and father and began living with them. The social worker even stated that she had not seen me smile or laugh in a long time, and seeing my interaction with the Breedlove's made her feel the family was a for sure fit for me.

On Wednesday, December 20, 1998, mother and father

adopted me, and I officially became Christopher L. Breedlove.

After I read through all the information, I couldn't help but feel more grateful for my parents. Just to see how much work they put in with me and how they stayed by my side. I cried and called both of my parents on the phone. I shared with them that I received my adoption papers and that I appreciated both of them. I genuinely felt unworthy of them as parents because I was such a challenging teenager with so many problems. My parents really were not the most emotional people, so I kept it brief and short and let them know that I was endlessly in gratitude to them.

Reading all of the papers that evening helped me understand my parents and their point of view in keeping the adoption under wraps. It made me have a higher respect for my parents and really showed how much they did love my sister and me in a weird way—weird because I felt that my parents loved me but were not trying to understand me except for blaming me. It wasn't fair for my family to blame me for bad relationships with other family members including them because they didn't want to discuss my past. A past in which I felt entitled to.

Adoptees really never get a chance to grieve the loss or separation from their birth mothers in the early stages of their lives. I think it's imperative for adoptees and adoptive parents to learn how to communicate with each other and the adoptive parents acknowledge the perspective of their adoptive child.

Background Checks

Dear Breedlove,

The next day I woke up constantly thinking about everything I read the night before. I ended up trying to search for my biological mother on Facebook and could not find her. I typed her full name and birthdate on Google and found two potential leads. I had to pay for a background check to get any information on her, and I paid the money and found multiple addresses. The two cell phone numbers provided on the background check were disconnected. I went out on a limb and drove to the address provided on whitepages.com.

| | | | | | | |

John

Dear Breedlove,

Not even 24 hours after receiving my adoption paperwork, I potentially located my biological mother. So, at 2:30 p.m. on March 28, 2017, I drove to Brenda's alleged home. I arrived around 3 p.m. and was very nervous. I had a printout of one of my adoption papers with her name as well as a printout of my baby feet ink prints just in case she wanted proof. I knocked on the door for about two minutes before I got a response. I audio recorded everything for my personal records. After two minutes of waiting, a man named John answered the door.

I asked him, "Is Brenda here?"
"Not at the moment," he said. "She's at work and won't be back until near five."
He added that I should come back the next day.
"I don't mean to put her business out there," I said, "but I think she is my biological mother.

"Christopher?"

"How do you know me?"

I was in disbelief that this person I didn't even know, knew of me.

I asked him how he knew my name, and he stated that Brenda talked about me all the time.

"Do you think she would want to see me?"

"Do you see me smiling right now? She would love to see you. Come back tomorrow."

I shook his hand, and we parted ways. That moment was so crazy to me just to know and confirm that my biological mother did live there, and I potentially might have found answers.

Waiting until the next day was killing me, so that evening, I took a shower and drove back to Brenda's house to meet her. I could not wait; I needed answers. I felt so uneasy and obsessed to the point I had to get it done.

When I arrived at Brenda's home for a second time, I hoped that she would be there.

Brenda

Dear Breedlove,

I arrived at about eight that evening.

Before I approached the door, I made sure I recorded the audio of what happened just for my records, and if my sister ever wanted any answers, I could present them to her. I set my phone to record and put it in the front pocket of my North Face jacket. I knocked on the door, and on the first knock, a woman answered the door. Initially, I was expecting my biological mother to be African American and my biological father to be Caucasian because that's what was stated in the adoption reports. A white woman answered the door instead.

"Is Brenda here?" I asked.

"I am Brenda."

I was in shock; *this* woman gave birth to me.

Initially, I thought she looked rough, but in her defense, she hadn't been off work for too long. She glared at me and looked stunned as to why I was on her doorstep, but she did ask me to come inside.

Before going any further, I had requested to see her driver's license so that she could confirm her identity. After she confirmed her identity, I just stared at her for about ten minutes and didn't say anything.

Awe and anger mingled insides of me.

"I don't know how to respond," I finally said.

"I know," she said. "It's been a long time. You will be 24 on April 29. I never forget your birthday. You know you have a sister, too?"

I nodded. "She's with me."

"No, my daughter Kristyn, she's 31. I had her before I had you, and she is here with me. She looks just like me. You are still so tiny, you were always so little. You know you were premature, right?"

It was the most bizarre feeling. I felt angry, betrayed, happy, sad, all at once. I had so many questions for her. She eventually asked me if I want to have a seat, and I did.

She went to shut the front door as I sat in the living room, and I asked her to keep the door open for my comfortability because I didn't trust her. We then migrated to her kitchen to start a conversation a long time in the making.

Let's Talk

I can recall nearly verbatim the conversation Brenda and I shared in the kitchen that night.

Me: I got the papers yesterday. I just want to take up 15 minutes of your time.

Brenda: Have a seat. You know you still have the same curly hair as when you were little.

Me: I'm sorry. I don't know how to feel. I'm hurt, upset, angry. I don't know how to respond.

Brenda: It was very hard for me then. I lost my parents, and all my kids were taken away from me.

Me: Did you know what I experienced after you left me?

Brenda: No.

Me: I was in one foster care home prior to being adopted, and I was physically abused there.

Brenda: Oh wow, I didn't know that happened to you. Your name was Christopher Anthony. You know that, right?

I disregarded her question.

Me: Do you know who the father is? Is he black or white?

Brenda: Your father was black, and he was a very attractive man. I was crazy about your father, but he didn't want to have anything to do with me or you. He was too focused on other girls. He is now married with kids.

She then gave me the full name of my biological father and what city he lived in along with his birthday.

Me: What drugs were you using? Did you use drugs while you were pregnant with me and my sister?

Brenda: No, I did not. Not with you or your older sister.

Me: Did you have any other children?

Brenda: No, I had two miscarriages and a set of twins that died, a boy and a girl.

Me: The female twin is my sister, and she is with me and alive. April 15 is her birthday.

Brenda: April 15, 1998. Oh my God, wow, I can't believe she is alive. I have one baby picture of you, my sister Judy has it though. Maybe I can send it to you.

Me: After I have all of my questions answered, I think we should resume our lives the way they were without being a part of it. I just needed these answers for me and my sister. For right now at least.

The irony with all of this is when I was away at university, there was this game called "Where is Brenda." Students would write the name Brenda in chalk around the entire campus. What were the odds that my biological mother's name would be Brenda?

Me: Why are you emotionless right now?

Brenda: It's been so long since I tried to find you.

Me: You tried to find me?

Brenda: Yes, for years. Even when you got older, I always tried Facebook. Do you have a Facebook?

Me: I'm not going to speak on that.

Brenda: Ok.

Me: I'm sorry if I'm coming off as rude or overly direct. I just don't know how to feel.

Brenda: I know.

Me: So, you just got so high one day and just left me and didn't come back for me?

Brenda: Yeah, it was a bad time for me. I thought of you every day. I had to dye my hair black because I had so many regrets about my life back then and stressed myself out. All of my hair used to be gray.

On the inside, I felt terrible that she felt that amount of stress in reference to me being out of her life all these years. However, I was still guarded because a part of me still fumed, which made me conflicted in how I should feel.

Me: What's your religion?

Brenda: Baptist.

Me: What are some health conditions you have in your family?

Brenda: COPD. That's from me smoking cigarettes.

I whipped out a small pad I had on me and began writing her responses down for each question I asked. I wasn't how long my phone would record for.

My birth mother stated that the twins were taken away from her because they found cocaine in her system. She said during her pregnancy with me she was a waitress at the IHOP on 8 Mile and Kelly Road, and she used to work a lot and had a rough pregnancy with me. All the children had different dads, same mother.

For the remainder of my conversation with my biological mother, I basically gave her a brief update of what I was doing in my life and reviewed all of the adoption papers with her. I let her know what happened to me after she left me.

Initially, I was VERY stern and direct with her. I didn't want to show any signs of weakness because I did not know what to expect, and I was also protecting myself from rejection.

I asked if there were any traumatic events that happened to me that I should know about, and she told me at six months I had a double hernia and had surgery for it. The next traumatic event she told me about was at a hotel with her boyfriend at the time named Daleon. We stayed at a hotel, and she said for some reason, I would not stop crying. Daleon was getting upset and yelled BE QUIET, but I did not.

Daleon then lit a cigarette and proceeded to put out the

cigarette on my arm. My biological mother said she had him arrested, and he did one year in jail for burning me, her 1-year-old child.

After I felt I got all the information I needed, I then asked her did she have questions, and she didn't. She said she was still adjusting to my presence, which was understandable.

I do believe that my conversation with her was needed because I wanted to be the bigger person, and I wanted to understand what happened to her and what frame of mind she was in when she was pregnant with me. I wanted to understand instead of withholding resentment and anger inside of me by holding on to the story of what I was told by my adoptive family and the adoption records.

Before parting, she asked me did I have social media, and I replied, "I think that is inappropriate right now." We also got on the topic of contact again, and I got her phone number and told her that I would be calling her, and she would not have direct access to me, and she would receive phone calls from an unknown or private caller because I wasn't ready to let her into my world—and wasn't sure if I'd ever be ready.

She then walked me to the door, and we talked about how good our meet and greet was, and she hugged me and said she loved me. I felt weird hearing those words. A part of believed the words were not genuine.
I just replied, "Ok, bye."

Undrey

Dear Breedlove,

After I left Brenda's place, I literally felt numb about everything. It was so much information to process. I just couldn't believe I received my papers one day, and the very next day, I located and met my biological mother the very next day—after 21 years. There was so much irony in this situation.

I kept rereading the papers and began researching information on my biological father. With Brenda's help and information, I actually found a lead and a person with the exact same spelling of the name he had as well as an address. On the fourth day of my self-discovery, I was on the search to find him.

When I reached the address later that afternoon, I was very frightened because I didn't know what to expect, but I had come this far, so I knew I wouldn't turn away. I knocked on the door, and he answered.

Me: Hey what's up, man? How are you doing?

He stared at me for a minute, puzzled.

Undrey: Good.
Me: Is your name Undrey?
Undrey: Yes.
Me: Do you mind if I get two minutes of your time?
Undrey: I don't mind.
Me: I know you have a wife and kids, but I found out I was adopted, and my mother was Brenda Diehr. It says that you were my putative biological father.

He took a step back and eyed me from top to bottom and back up.

Undrey: Who are you?

Me: My name is Christopher, and my mother's name was Brenda.

Undrey: Come in, Come on. How you doing?

Me: Good, thank you.

He said my name and Brenda's name over and over, as if recalling them aloud would clarify everything in his mind.

Me: Do you mind if I see your ID? I just want to make sure you are who you say you are.

Quickly, he left and returned with his ID; he was definitely Undrey.

Undrey: I have been praying about this.

He began to shut the door, and I asked him to keep it open because, just like with Brenda, I was scared and didn't know what to expect from him.

Undrey: I am Undrey, and I just want to explain the relationship between Brenda and me. She was married at the time, and her and I were involved and knew each other from work. At the time I wasn't sure if you were my child because she was married. You are an answer to my prayer, and this is weird that this happened.

Me: Do you want to do a paternity test?

Undrey: Yes, I do.

Me: I think we look alike. I noticed so many similarities looking at you. I feel like you are my biological father

Undrey: I feel like that, too, It's weird that all of this is happening after so long.

I shared with him all of the information I had learned within the past couple of days and how it all eventually led to him.

Undrey: I tried to find out information on what happened to you, and I did receive a letter indicating that you were my son. It said I had a son named Christopher. And they stated that they didn't have me as the legal father, and I couldn't get any information. I asked Brenda what happened to you, and she said that you were taken from her. How did you feel when you saw her?

Me: I'm still processing everything, honestly. It makes me feel good to understand what happened those three years that I couldn't account for. I just want to understand. This feels like a movie

Undrey: It is not a movie. It's reality. You know I really see her in you. I also have been praying because I did want to know if I had a child out there, and I did, I would want to see him. You are an answer to my prayer. I have no excuses, and I'm not making any excuses for anything. This is the truth, and this situation is what it is. And I would like to get a paternity test to confirm you are my son. I would like to know.

Me: Ok, I understand. I will reach back out in a few days. Do you have a phone number? Just a heads-up, I will be contacting you on unknown or private numbers just like Brenda.

I watched as he began writing his phone number down.

Me: Could I take a photo of you? I I always wanted to know what you looked like.

Undrey: Can I give you a picture, or send you one? I look rough right now.

Me: Could you give me a picture? I think you look nice right now actually.

Undrey: I think you look nice, too.

He then changed his mind and allowed me to take the picture. I pulled out my phone and a took a burst of pictures.

Me: This is all still so crazy to me. I received my papers Monday, met Brenda Tuesday, processed everything on Wednesday, and met you on Thursday.

Undrey: I don't know what to say.

Me: Well I'm going to get going here, I will contact you about a paternity test, and we can go from there.

Undrey: Okay. It was nice meeting you, and I hope you don't feel any negative ways about me. See you soon.

| | | | | | | |

Paternity Test

Dear Breedlove,

After my conversation with Undrey, I really did want to hurry and take care of the paternity test to confirm everything. I purchased a kit from Rite Aid for about $25, and he paid the $90 lab fee. The lab results would take about three weeks to process.

We decided to meet at Starbucks. We talked for about three hours about random things and the story of how everything happened. I told him about what happened to me prior to being adopted and shared my progress from then until now. He began crying, and I comforted him, and I started crying, too. I remember my body jolting with emotions. I cannot fully express the intensity of that moment. I took note of his sincerity.

About an hour into our conversation, a man who was sitting closely to us had said, "This right here made me smile. And not to impede, but you guys don't need a paternity test to prove anything. I think it shows," and walked away. We continued talking, and Undrey said that when he returned home, he would set up a Dropbox account and send me some photos from back in the day.

He actually kept his word, and three hours after we met, he sent me over 300 photos of different biological family members and photos of him as well as my brothers and sisters. It was so overwhelming but interesting at the same time. I decided to give Undrey my phone number because we really did connect. I felt like I trusted him a little more and had less resentment with him opposed to my biological mother. I felt so much anger with the both of them, but a little more with her.

We took the cotton swabs and did the DNA test, and we were both equally as excited. The biggest thing that stuck out was how humble he was. My biological father had said, "I am unworthy of this moment. I am amazed by your grace about this situation. This is nothing but God's favor."

| | | | | | | |

More Diehr's

Dear Breedlove,

I remember the day I met more people on my birth mothers' side. On March 31, 2017, I called Brenda to confirm that we were still on for 3:30 p.m. Brenda asked me did I like spaghetti. And I said yes. Prior to leaving, I only had $2.40 in my bank account because I lost my job two weeks prior because of a prolonged interview for a show I was auditioning for during my lunch break. I spent my last $2.40 on one gallon of gas to meet my sister and to see Brenda again.

I arrived at Brenda's home for the second time since first meeting her just a few days ago. Brenda answered the door along with her brother who is my uncle
Terry and my older biological sister. I remember thinking that this might be more than I could handle.

I excused myself for acting weird because I did not know how to respond. Initially, I just stared at everyone in the room, and I stayed quiet for a few minutes, analyzing everyone's facial features. I was in awe that these people resembled me so much. ESPECIALLY Terry and my older sister. We all began talking, and they all commented on how I looked the same from when I was one years old.

Uncle Terry: You were a demon baby. You used to throw your bottle at me all the time.
Brenda: You used to wake me up in the middle of the night and hit me with a bottle to let me know you wanted more milk. It's a miracle that this even happened.
Uncle Terry: It really is.

After we began catching up, I remained very brief on the information I disclosed because I still wanted to protect my adoptive family. All of my answers initially were not necessarily truthful because I wanted to remain private about some things, such as what city I lived and where my family was and questions like that. I wanted to also protect my sister.

There were a few brief pauses for a while, and I took that time to ask about my baby pictures. All three of them responded and said there was only ONE picture they had of me as a baby. Before April 1, 2017, I have NEVER seen a picture of what I looked like as a baby. My sister Kristyn went upstairs for a few minutes, looked through her things, and brought down my one and only baby picture. When she gave it to me, I just stared in awe of how beautiful I was as a baby. I looked on the back of the baby picture, and it had my birthday written on it as well as my first given name: *Christopher Anthony Diehr.*

In the midst of all of us talking, my nephew was also there. His name was Benjamin, and he was 7 years old. I remember laughing because he locked himself in the bathroom because he was very shy initially. After a while, he opened the door and invited me in his room, and I asked him, "Do you know who I am"?

"Yes, my mom's brother."

"Yes, I am. I am your Uncle Chris. Nice to meet you, Ben."

After I walked out of his room and asked my biological sister could we go for a walk and talk in private, she agreed and grabbed her jacket because it was chilly outside. We went for a 45-minute walk if not longer. I had so many questions. The first question I asked was why was she with Brenda and not me.

Kristyn: Mom left me, too, when I was nine years old. I ended up going to live with my biological dad who forbade me to see Mom until I was 18 years old. Up until that point, Mom and I wrote letters to each other. After I graduated high school, I sought Mom out and been around ever since. It took me some time to get over things and want to build a relationship again with her.

Me: Wow, that makes me feel a little better. Before knowing your story with Brenda, I was jealous of you because I was under the impression that you were kept, and my sister and I were not.

Kristyn: There is no need to have been jealous or be jealous. You seemed like you turned out really good.

We then began to walk closer. I placed my hand around her shoulder as she placed her hand around my waist as we began firing away with more questions. For some reason, I felt an intensely strong connection with my sister. On our way back home, Uncle Terry was on his way out and drove over a few streets to find my sister and I walking to say goodbye. I asked him for a photo with him because I was still in awe of my resemblance to him, and afterwards, he drove off. My sister and I were almost back at Brenda's home at this point and before we went in, I asked to take a picture with her because the lighting was really good outside.

Kristyn: It is so good seeing you after 21 years.
Me: It is, sister.

My sister and I hugged for a few minutes and went back into Brenda's home to eat. At first, I was VERY hesitant to eat anything that Brenda prepared because I was still suspicious of her. But after a while, I did eventually get hungry and decided to make myself a plate of spaghetti, and it was actually really good. The funny part about it being good is it actually tasted JUST like my mom's spaghetti. It was so good I ended up having two full portions.

After I ate, I made an effort to get to know my nephew for a little bit. He started off very shy but opened up VERY quickly. He started off showing me all of his favorite toys. He was such a character. He randomly stumbled across his Captain America Halloween suit, and he actually put on the entire suit, mask included, and pretended he was Captain America. I was totally entertained and ran with his whole performance.

Eventually, 8:30 p.m. came around, and I thought it was getting late, so I said my goodbyes and left. But before I left, I asked for a picture with Brenda and my sister Kristyn together. When I looked at that picture, I found it crazy how strong the resemblance was.

I said my goodbyes and left. After I left, I felt confused and overwhelmed with emotions. It was hard for me to vent about anything because my mother and father were not receptive to listening. In those moments, I knew that I had to compartmentalize and continue to be open to the experience in understanding my past and my birth parents.

| | | | | | |

Arrows

Dear Breedlove,

During the process of interacting with both of my birth parents separately, I noticed that Undrey and I had been getting along. I liked how he called frequently to check on me to see how I was doing. I remember Brenda said that he would have been doubtful about engaging with me, but he was the opposite. Growing up, my dad and I had a distant relationship. It was kind of warming to have a father figure calling me just to talk to me. Despite the fact I knew that there was guilt there from years of not being there, the feeling felt nice.

For my third interaction, I remember Undrey and I going bowling. At first, I was apprehensive because I felt bad for hanging out with my birth father. I felt like I was disloyal to my adoptive father, but I was curious at the same time.

Undrey and I bowled about four games. Of course, Undrey kicked my ass in bowling. Despite the fact he nailed me in the game of bowling, I actually learned how to bowl correctly.

Bowling Tip 101: look at the arrows when you bowl, not the pins.

Triangles & Starbucks

Dear Breedlove,

My birth parents were not together or currently coupled. My birth father was married, and my birth mother was in a relationship. They hadn't seen each other in over 21 years. I decided to orchestrate a meeting with my birth parents at Starbucks at a location near me. During my bowling session with Undrey, he had requested that he see Brenda because he had something to say to the both of us.

We all arrived around the same time and began walking toward Starbucks. We immediately sat down, and it was awkward for a few seconds. Undrey then lightened the mood. We all began talking about how crazy the situation was. Undrey began apologizing to Brenda for not believing that I was his biological son. They both began apologizing to me for not being there.

In that moment, I had asked them what did they want from me. They both had said they wanted a relationship.

I responded that I kind of did, too, and we should communicate and leave it at that. There was a natural, unforced connection with the both of them. We talked at Starbucks for about two hours and left the parking lot and took some photos together. After I got in my car, I thought it was pretty cool that we all got to sit down together despite our unsavory past. It made me feel loved that they both wanted a relationship with me.

| | | | | | |

Siblings

Dear Breedlove,

During the process of uncovering all of my roots and meeting so many people, I decided to continue unveiling and meeting more of my blood, despite the fact the DNA test results were still pending.

Undrey and I continued to keep in contact, and on one meet up, I four out of six of my half-siblings. When I was younger, I used to always want more siblings. And to realize that all together, I had eight siblings in total was shocking to me.

Since I was the one to pick a restaurant, I chose Red Lobster, a restaurant that was convenient for everyone. We all arrived, and of course, I was running a few minutes behind, per usual. As I arrived and parked, Undrey approached my car with his camera, and he began taking pictures of the moments. Undrey loved bringing his camera places to capture moments.

The first sibling I remember meeting on Undrey's side was my brother Anthony. We hugged for a few minutes. I then met one of my sisters and her daughter at the dinner as well as my brother Bren. As soon as I met my sister Undreya, we hugged, and I felt like I have known her for ages, that's how comfortable I felt with her. Fortunately, all of the siblings were not present all at once because it was a lot for me to take in.

Shortly after, I met my second oldest sister Chante'. I remember we all enjoyed our food despite the fact we had a waiter who was throwing hell of shade. Meeting my siblings on my birth dad's side was a nerve-racking experience in the beginning, but I eventually got comfortable. I enjoyed how our connections just flowed, and nothing was forced. I have always kept a small group of friends, so it was exciting to me to bond with my siblings and learn about them, their lives and experiences. Funny part about it was growing up when I started questioning my past, I used to have feelings that something more was out there. I felt like I had more siblings aside from my sister whom I grew up with, and I did.

Reflection Point

Over the course of getting to know my birth parents, I found it very difficult to maintain relationships with all my siblings, too, because I was still overwhelmed. I wasn't accustomed to people contacting me frequently or daily because I didn't even have that type of relationship with my own family. So it was a major adjustment for me.

Even as I look back on my story, I felt as if God gave me this story to restore balance in both of my parents' lives —birth and adoptive. I often would think of myself as a centerpiece of a scale, wavering back and forth. I was the central point in providing balance in combining both of my families. My story was about all of us. I thought of my story in the eyes of us all being spirits needing healing.

|||||||

Recharge

Dear Breedlove,

After almost two weeks, I had several interactions with both of my birth parents and met quite a few people. I felt like I needed a "recharge" day, a day where I just sat in my thoughts and processed the information that I uncovered. I felt like I was just going and going and going without processing anything at all.

On that recharging day, I reflected on my parents and thought I had understood why they did what they did. I understood they were trying to protect me and my sister from more feelings of being unwanted. I even understood how my sister could view the adoption much differently than I could. Growing up, my sister always felt that by me informing her of her adoptive past I was making her choose to be on my side and hate our family.

My sister viewed things differently because she was adopted at four days old and was raised as a newborn. I, on the other hand, had three years of memories that nobody could explain to me. I remembered names and people who were not around.

| | | | | | | |

Paternity Results

Dear Breedlove,

So after almost two weeks of waiting, I finally received the paternity results between my alleged biological father and me. On the day I received the results, I went to Brenda's because I wanted to review the results in front of her. I remember getting off the phone with customer service, and after almost two weeks of waiting, they said my results were available. I logged into my account online for Identigene, and the first thing I read was "The alleged biological father is NOT excluded."
Instantly, my heart dropped.
"May I be excused?" I said.

I walked to my car and sat down in front of Brenda's driveway just staring at the results. Trying to figure out did I read something wrong. Should I call for a second DNA test? I started crying because I interpreted the results as "he was not my birth father." I spent time with this man's family, I met his children. I felt angry with Brenda for not coming correctly with facts.

I was so frustrated about the situation I had to vent about it. So, I called my best friend Bianca to reveal the results to her. She asked me to email her the results, and moments later, she said, "Chris, where did you get *not* the father from? It says 99.9999997% that he's the biological father."

After I analyzed the results again and read what "not excluded" actually, meant along with the percentage, I realized the test affirmed that Undrey was my biological father. At this point, I was mad at myself for crying over nothing.

I went back inside with Brenda and shared the results again for a second time with Brenda and Kristyn, and we all laughed at how I incorrectly read the data. I felt so embarrassed about not paying attention to the percentage.

Hey, first time for everything, right?

| | | | | | | |

Judy Who?

Dear Breedlove,

For the first few weeks after meeting my birth parents, I thought my birth mother was calling me too much. It was irritating initially. I still had mixed feelings about everything. I started to feel bad for even talking to my birth family. I didn't want my parents thinking that I loved them any less because I had curiosities. Dealing with all the pressures of finding by birth family and dealing with it alone caused me to have shifty mood swings.

A few days before my birthday, Brenda called me four times. After the fifth time, I answered. She asked me if I wanted to meet my aunt Judy and she said that my aunt used to watch me when I was 3.

At first, I responded, "No" because I was overwhelmed

from meeting so many people. Of course, I had a change of heart, so I agreed to meet my Aunt Judy.

Due to my car being repossessed, I needed rides. I did not want my biological family knowing my whereabouts or leads on my sister. My biggest focus was protecting her in everything that I did. I remained private about my actual last name as well as her identity. Brenda picked me up at Trader Joe's near me. I told them that the Trader Joe's was a central halfway point of where I really stayed, but actually, I lived down the street.

After about a 20-minute drive, we arrived at a hospital. Brenda and my sister told me that Aunt Judy used to watch me along with Uncle Mike when I was 3. Prior to seeing my Aunt Judy, I was told that she had an aggressive form of lung cancer, and she was on morphine and bed rest.

The elevator rang. We arrived on floor four.

I felt nervous the closer we got to Aunt Judy's room. I didn't know what to expect. Brenda and Kristen walked in first and introduced me, saying, "Look who we have" before cueing in for me to walk in the hospital room.

"Oh my God," Aunt Judy stated. "It is really you."

I sat there, staring blankly at her because in my head I was thinking, *I have no idea who you are, and I don't know you.* I felt so uncomfortable.

We stayed in Aunt Judy's room for a while. Aunt Judy couldn't talk much because she was in a lot of pain. Shortly after, a family cousin named Melanie came in. She introduced herself to me and said that she was glad to meet me. After our brief introduction, I ended up overhearing a conversation she was having with Brenda about how her husband fainted and had syncope. This cued my interest because growing up I had random fainting spells. According to Google, it's called syncope.

I asked Brenda and Kristyn could I leave to talk with Melanie more about her husband's condition. Melanie told me that syncope ran on my birth mothers' side of the family. When she said that, everything made sense to me. For years, I had tried to solve the mystery of what the "bodily jitters, or fainting spells" were, and now I was provided with answers. I have had heart scans performed, neurology tests, and none could figure out why these episodes occurred. When I returned to Aunt Judy's room, we all said our goodbyes to her. On our way out, she said "I love you all."

| | | | | | |

Death on My Birthday

Dear Breedlove,

I remember feeling so excited about my birthday. I wanted to make a big change. I was still on a high from a fashion show that I did the day before. I woke up on my birthday around
11 a.m. to a phone call from my birth mother, and I missed the first phone call, and she called me again.
I answered, "Good morning."
She responded, "Happy birthday and enjoy your day."
We talked for a few minutes, and as we parted, she told me that Aunt Judy passed at 1:30 a.m. on my birthday.

Even though I barely knew who she was or remembered who she was for that matter, it was sad to me. In a way, I was upset for Brenda telling me on my birthday that somebody died on my day of birth. Like come on. But Brenda apologized for doing that and thought that I should know. She told me the viewing was on Tuesday and the funeral would be Wednesday and extended an offer to go. She stated my other aunts, uncles, and cousins would be so excited to see me.

As soon as she said that, I felt weird. I didn't want to meet any more people. I was barely processing that she was my birth mother. I told her that I would let her know because I was unsure.

As weird as it sounded, I thought it was so bizarre that I met and saw Aunt Judy after 21 years for the first time, and she died four days later on my birthday. Maybe I am overly superstitious, but I found so much irony in that situation.

| | | | | | |

Sleeping Judy

Dear Breedlove,

I decided to go with Brenda and Kristyn. I never saw a dead body before so I thought It would be interesting if I went. I felt nervous because there were more family members there to meet, and I didn't want to meet any more people.

Of course, I was being kind and courteous to everyone, but in my head, I was thinking, *Is this awkward for anyone?*

As the viewing ended, everyone began saying their final goodbyes to her body. As I approached her dead body, I felt awkward because in a way I didn't remember her, but apparently she used to watch me when I was 3." I placed my hand over her forehead and felt her cold, lifeless body. I ran my fingers through her reddish-brown hair. Then, I sat in disbelief as I came to the realization of my own mortality. Internally, I began to really appreciate being alive.

As Brenda drove to our meeting spot, my mind was in a somber mood, thinking about the viewing, seeing the body, and how it all made me feel. When Brenda asked me if I wanted to come to the funeral, I told her no because it was too much for me. I was pretty shaken about seeing a dead body and placing my hand on one, too.

Seeing a dead body for the first time stunned me. I could barely sleep when I got home and spent my entire night tossing and turning. I woke up at 4:30 a.m., still unable to sleep as I thought about Aunt Judy's body. Even though I didn't really remember who she was, I didn't remember going to a funeral either, so I thought why not go to Aunt Judy's. I messaged Brenda, telling her I changed my mind, and I wanted to go to the funeral.

At the funeral, just like the viewing, I felt so out of place and awkward seeing all the people cry and get emotional. It was hard for me to be empathetic because I didn't know who Aunt Judy was.

So many of the family members were fascinated to meet me. It was overwhelming to hear "Oh, here is your cousin," "This is your uncle dahaaa da da da..." My mind felt confused because in my head, I thought, *but I already have cousins*, and I had no idea who these people were.

After the funeral, there was a luncheon. We all went, and it was actually fairly enjoyable. I was able to get more answers, and I was able to talk to my entire birth family. They had a similar humor as I did, and I did find myself feeling really comfortable at times. At the luncheon, I learned that I was a first-generation college student on my birth mother's side. I thought that was pretty cool.

| | | | | | | |

Outspoken

Dear Breedlove,

Today, I just wanted to sit and process everything, again. These past few days had been crazy. Around noon, Brenda called me, asking could she take me to dinner for my birthday. Even though my birthday was a few days ago, and I didn't want to leave the house, I knew she was going through a rough time with the passing of her sister, and I felt bad, so I agreed.

We met at our pick-up spot and went to Red Coat Tavern. She ordered chicken tenders, and I ordered this monstrous burger which was pretty good. At this dinner, I brought my adoption files with me as well as some photos of myself when I was younger for her to see. When I showed her some of the adoption papers, I made sure none of the papers had my parents' information on it or my real last name because my main focus was protecting my sister and family.

She kept apologizing for not being there and she asked me, "Why do you keep calling me Brenda?" I felt so bad being so blunt with her, but I told her that I would never call her mother because my parents were the only two people deserving of being called mother and father. "I will call you by your first name Brenda." I told her that they deserved to have something for raising me for over 18 years. I also told her that she may never get the satisfaction of meeting my sister because she was raised as an infant and had no memories of the past.

She said that she understood and wanted me around in her life and that I made her happy. She seemed to disconnect for a little after I said that to her. She started to look down more during our conversation over dinner. As we left and parted ways, she gave me a card for my birthday, and I thanked her.

For some reason, when she was emotional toward me, I didn't like it. I even told her that despite the fact I found her and my birth father, I wanted that same love that they were trying to give me from my mother and father who raised me. I wanted my adoptive family to have interest in who I was as a person as opposed to just knowing me as the child they raised.

| | | | | | |

Force

Dear Breedlove,

After three months of keeping my secret of finding and locating both of my birth parents from my parents, I finally told them. I remember feeling nervous, and I called my mother first, and I shared the story with her. I wanted her to feel at ease and not hurt. So, I told her how much I loved her and how much I appreciated her, and my reasons for searching for my birth parents had nothing to do with her, and I wanted to reiterate that because I did love my mother. My mother thanked me for sharing my story; however, she said that from that moment forward, she did not want to discuss anything regarding the adoption or my birth parents. My father had a similar reaction he basically stated that it wasn't any of his business and chose to not discuss it either.

Apart of me understood where they were coming from, and the other half was hurt. I felt that these people were essentially a part of who I was, and I wanted my parents to talk

to me about the knowledge that I learned about my life before I was adopted. Out of respect to them, I kept my thoughts, views, feelings on my biological parents private.

Roughly three months went by, and I felt so much pressure to tell my sister the truth about us being adopted after my mother lied to her a few years ago by denying the adoption. For some reason, whenever I talked about the adoption with my parents, it made me angry, so my approach about the matter was always disrespectful and condescending. I admit to not being so nice when talking about the matter. But to me, I felt like I was the adult in the situation. My parents kept saying that they didn't want to talk about the adoption nor did they understand why I kept bringing up the past. But in my eyes, it made me angry to know that NOBODY wanted to talk about the truth. Their excuse was "We are not ready to talk about it." I grew to a point of feeling like "I'm tired of sweeping stuff under the rug. I wanted everything to be brought to light instead of being ignored."

With every excuse they made, I thought, *How are you not ready?*

I wasn't ready for several family members to throw my adoptive past in my face, but I had to address it. Sometimes in life, there are things that you are not ready for you that you have to blatantly face. I remained quiet about the matter for a few months.

On one particular day, I was angry, and I was not coming from a place of sincerity but hurt. At the time I was envious of my mother and sister's relationship, and I did want to hurt them all because I felt emotionally tainted by my family. I remember calling my mother and telling her that I was going to tell my sister that I found our birth mother.

My mother responded, "You want to make threats? I can make threats, too. If you tell her, I will burn everything that you have in my home."

I was LIVID.

After she hung up, I called her back and left nasty

voicemails. I called her back, and she sent me to voicemail, to which I said, "I dare you, bitch, to burn my things."

Afterwards, I called my dad, letting him know the same thing. I just didn't feel it was right for my relationship with my sister to suffer because my parents did not want to be honest about me and my sister's adoptive past.

I didn't think it was fair for my parents to blame my odd and distant relationship with my sister on me when in actuality a percentage of it was their fault for making me look like I was lying about the adoption when I was actually right.

I'm still assuming that my parents thought that my delivery of our adoptive past to my sister was going to be harsh or hurtful because of how they thought I viewed the adoption.

But in fact, I did otherwise. I took it upon myself to call my sister, and we chatted for a few minutes.

We started off catching up seeing as I hadn't spoken to her for a few weeks.

After catching up, I asked her, "Do you believe me?"

"Believe you about what?"

"You know what I'm talking about."

"No, Chris, I don't believe you."

My heart dropped and twisted. I felt so hurt that my own sister didn't believe me and she thought I was making up things to tear her away from our family. In my mind, that made me think, what does my sister really think of me?

It even made me question my intentions as to why I wanted her to know.

After she expressed not believing me, I decided to let it go.

Roughly two weeks passed, and my sister rejecting the truth just ATE at me. So, I decided to randomly text her everything. I sent her photos of my birth mother and our older sister Kristyn. And in the text, I told her how much I loved her and that our parents saved our lives from a life that could have been disastrous for us both. I shared with her my interactions with them, and I told her I wanted her to know the truth because nobody was going to tell her. I felt since I found out at 17 years old, it was only appropriate and fair for her to have knowledge about it at the age of 19.

I felt the longer the secret was held, the harder it would be for her to deal with, and I knew because I myself experienced it.

Her response?

I understand it was different for you because you were adopted at the age of three, but I was adopted as a baby, so Mom and Dad are all that I know. I don't care about those people, nor do I care about a relationship with them. I'm glad you found out where you came from, but this is where I came from. Mom and Dad gave us everything we ever wanted, and you should be more grateful. I don't want to hear it from you. I want to hear it from Mom and Dad when they are ready to talk about it.

After reading my sister's response, I felt overwhelmed and taken aback of how mature her response was, and after that, I didn't care about the adoption stuff anymore knowing that my sister finally knew the truth, whether she wanted to believe it or not.

Reflection Point

What this situation with my sister taught me was to stop forcing the truth on people. Some people are ready to face the truth, and some people view the truth as painful. It is in my nature to solve things or problems quickly, and when people don't have the same view in solving problems, sometimes, I get pushy. However, this situation made me consider how I could go about changing being so forceful.

I had to ask myself why was I being so forceful in my family facing the truth. The whole saying of "the truth will first piss you off, and then set you free" is so accurate in reflecting on my life events. It hurt me to see people who I loved drifting away from me because of my lack of control and intense emotions regarding the adoption.

Not to justify my forceful nature in trying to get my parents to talk about my adoption, but I was forceful about it because I thought it was important as a family to address issues and heal each other. I also know that time is not always promised, and I felt like my family didn't want to solve our family issues, and they kept putting our healing off because they didn't want to deal with. I wanted my family to be grounded in my love for them and understand the importance of my birth family without feeling threatened or assuming my emotions toward them because of their insecurities.

Perhaps my sister didn't want to know because she was raised as an infant, and I was 4 years old, so I had memories, and all she knew were my parents and respecting her view. Perhaps my parents didn't want to disclose the information to my sister because maybe they felt if my reactions were terrible maybe my sister's reaction would be the same or worse. That thought led them to be fearful of potentially losing or being emotionally distant toward another one of their children.

Dichotomous

Dear Breedlove,

Over the course of getting to know my birth parents, I struggled greatly in trying not to compare my parents with my biological parents. For example, with my parents we didn't really talk on the phone that much. I always wanted a close relationship with my family where we communicated daily and got to know each other personally because I always felt like my parents didn't really know who I was. Meanwhile, my biological parents were so engaged in trying to understand and know who

I was by calling me every few days to check in and set days to spend time with me. I understood that they were trying to make up for lost time; it was the principle.

Sometimes, I found myself saying, "Wow, my birth mom is calling and texting me every day good morning and goodnight," and I wanted that same thing from my mother. Soon after meeting my birth father, he would pick me up and hug me and say, "I love you, Chris," which was something that I yearned for from my father who raised me. When I would go in for hugs with my adoptive father, he would stick his hand out and request a handshake instead. That always made me feel less than or unworthy of his love due to him being uncomfortable with my sexual fluidity. I started feeling like I had a double life, and I felt like I was cheating on my parents by even entertaining my birth parents.

Reflection Point

Throughout this process, I have learned to accept all parties involved as they are and tried to understand everyone's story because there are always multiple sides to a story. I didn't want to discriminate against my birth mother for the story of her being a drug addict, nor did I want to discriminate against my birth father because he was out of the picture and disregarded me as his biological child. I wanted to understand the WHY in their stories as opposed to being angry with them. The fact that my biological parents both acknowledged my emotions and apologized for their wrongdoings healed my anger with the both of them. The biggest struggle for me throughout this process was that I felt guilty for pursuing what I viewed as a blessing because it was hurting other people whom I loved. I then realized that I couldn't let my parents take away my joy of discovering who I am and finding the additional pieces to parts of me.

| | | | | | |

Six-Month Update

Dear Breedlove,

Six months after my brief interaction with my biological parents, I continued to remain in contact with them. Before, I felt very stand offish, and I didn't really care to know them because I was fearful. And in a way, I never imagined myself even finding both of them. In my head, the story I was told about my birth mother being a drug addict had me believing she was probably dead. The same was true in regard to the mysterious unknown of my father. Even when my birth father asked me what I wanted, I told him that I wasn't sure because I thought that they were both dead. But I pushed myself over the past few months to learn a lot about my birth parents.

Reflection Point

It is so very important to challenge the information you receive.

If I had not challenged the information provided to me about my biological mother's incarceration, I would have never continued my search. After in-depth research, I learned my birth mother was never incarcerated. I was able to locate both of my birth parents after 21 years in four days using background checks.

Side note: The papers had the race of my birth parents mixed up. My birth mother was Caucasian, and my birth father was African American. I think it is important for social workers and adoption agencies to document clear, concise, and accurate information on records regarding adoptees.

I also had a friend who found her birth mother after 20 years. In her papers, it said her mother passed away; however, she ended up locating her birth mother on her own.

I'm sharing pieces of my story to motivate other adoptees to keep trying until you find answers to your questions and continue to seek the answers you deserve. Throughout my journey as an adoptee, I have grown more passionate about understanding the mind of an adoptee. Recently, I conducted an online survey with over 50-plus participants. The survey had a series of questions for adoptees to answer, ranging from questions about closed adoptions, ethnicities, and their relationships with their adoptive families. The results showed that over 35 percent of adoptees coming from an African-American family had their adoptive past kept private or hidden from them.

I think sometimes as people in general we want to protect our families or loved ones from things that may hurt them. As an adoptee to adoptive parents in the black community and the adoption community, not disclosing your child's adoptive past could be a great hinderance to their mental health and a decrease in trust with the adoptive parent(s). There have also been several studies in which there has been a rise in mental illness when these things are not openly discussed with adoptees. Disclosing your child's adoptive status is necessary for them to live a life rooted in truth and reality.

|||||||

Pretty Princess, Tight Jeans, and Jail

Dear Breedlove,

For the past few months, things had been settled, but I was bothered more that my sister's adoptive past was out, yet my parents were still not addressing it. It's as if they were okay with me taking the blame that I wanted to taint my sisters' image of our family. I could NOT let go nor be quiet about the subject. I even began thinking about my sister's words more—of her wanting my parents to tell her of her adoptive past, but they never had the intent on doing so. It made me question were my feelings ever going to be validated in regard to the adoption and that I was being truthful in the situation regarding my sister.

I stayed at my adoptive mother's house for a few days before I went to move out of state to repair things with my on and off again partner Durabi for the second time. I needed a place to stay for about a week. My mother and I have always had a rocky relationship because we were both so outspoken.

It was my third day being at my mother's house, and I began reflecting on the relationships I had with my family, and I felt like my family was unreliable during times when I needed something. In addition to feeling like I was a burden to them, somehow, yet again, my sister and I got into a disagreement about "getting over the past." Getting over the past was something that I have always struggled with. To me, the past meant so much because I believed that there was so much to learn from the past, but somehow, I always found myself to be stuck in the past about other people's past actions toward me because I felt guilty about how I was reacting to their actions in the past. In addition to my reactions, whether they be good or bad, the disagreement went from talking about the past to misunderstandings regarding the adoption.

Originally, the whole disagreement was about getting a ride somewhere because at the time I didn't have a car. But when other people needed something in the family, I was the first to offer my help if I could. Any who, I remember getting extremely passionate during this particular disagreement with my sister. I felt like my sister didn't understand how I was trying to help her by telling her the truth of her story, too.

Despite the fact I disclosed the story to her twice and my sister only slightly acknowledged our adoption, it still bothered me that my parents were not acknowledging their dishonesty in telling my sister that I was not being honest in disclosing her adoptive past. I felt like I wanted to be heard by my parents; I

didn't like the adoption being off limits to talk about. The comment I remember the most that hurt was that I was trying to tear our family apart and that I was disrespectful.

She didn't understand how it felt for people to make threats to me for concealing the truth from my own sister and how much those threats hurt me when they came from my parents.

"You will cause a rift in your relationship with us if you tell your sister."

"I will burn your things if you do."

"We are trying to protect 'our' child."

"You're adopted, she is not."

"Tell your truth, not other people's."

I felt that she was of age to understand. I didn't want family members randomly dropping hints to her about the adoption how it was done to me. I wanted it to be delivered in a warm way to where she understood and didn't feel hurt and confused like I did. To this day, sometimes I felt like my sister never really understood her importance to me. I would never lie to her or try to tear her down even though I was envious of her relationship with my mother and father. Inside, I felt like I went through all the work to get my answers from my past as well as hers if she ever wanted to know. Internally, I felt offended of what was coming from my sister's mouth, and I threw a water bottle at her out of rage, and of course I missed. Not a big metal water bottle. a half-filled plastic bottle (not to justify my actions). I was angry in that moment because I was concealing all of those things that were said to me in an effort to conceal the truth from her and protect my parents' image in her eyes.

Of course, my sister, being the Aries that she is, threw the bottle back. As a family member came by to pick me up to defuse the situation between my sister and I, my mother made a surprise home visit on her lunch break.

My mother has always been speedy when it came to the topic of "my sister's adoption." She immediately pulled into the driveway and got out of her car, and as I was leaving with my aunt, she told me that I couldn't get my belongings out of her house. She did what she did best: threaten me to quiet me. Of course, the underlying motive was because I talked about the adoption subject with my sister, and my mother still wasn't ready to face the matter with my sister.

After my mother said that, I got out of the car and raced to the door because my mother was petty, and half the time she was serious. I needed my things because I did freelance work from home to make my money, and I also needed meds for my dog from his neutering. We both raced to the door while I had my dog in my hand. As she held the door, I shoved her with the right side of my hip, and she shoved back. She then began yelling, "Chris is punching me."

After I realized my mother was verbally lying on me, I grew extremely angry because I felt betrayed. I then pointed my finger in her face and told her that she needed to tell the truth and stop hiding it, and I snatched her winter hat off of her head. I understood I was being the aggressor in some way, but my feelings regarding the adoption were ignored for so long. I had a lot of built up resentment toward my parents due to them not being forthcoming with my sister.

My aunt Sue then got out of her car and stood with my mother and tried to defuse the situation yet again. After my mother threatened to call the police, she pulled out her phone and dialed. I grew fearful because my mother was just yelling I punched her when I didn't.

So, I knocked the phone out of her hand, and as I did, my mother yelled, "Sue, Chris is punching me." From my aunt's angle of where she was standing, it did appear that way, but in reality, I hit the phone out of her hand. My aunt then grabbed a metal grocery basket that was in the garage and began hitting me with it and said, "Don't hit my sister. GET OUTTA HERE." I couldn't believe that happened and began to walk

around the apartment complex with my dog. As I walked, I heard my mother calling the police. In the distance I heard, "Help, a strange man is punching me."

As I circled around, three police cars pulled onto my mother's property. As I approached the condo, two police officers began questioning me, asking me my side of the story. I was honest, and I admitted to shoving her and knocking the phone out of her hand. My aunt and my mother made statements. My sister came out, and she looked confused as to why the police were at our house, and my mother asked her to go back inside the house. I heard my mother bring up my mental illness into the conversation with the police as well. I felt like my mother was coming after the progress that I was making for myself emotionally and mentally. I was attending therapy and working on healing myself. She used everything she knew about me against me to fit her case.

After I was questioned, I remember hearing, "You have somewhere to put your dog?" I began crying because I was super attached to my dog, even though I knew he was in good hands and kept safe with my sister. The police then arrested me. I thought to myself in the back of the police car that I didn't even hit her, why was I being arrested.

All of this because of the "adoption" subject."

As the police pulled off, I remember seeing my mother get in her car and return to work. If she was so hurt or felt so threatened, where was the evidence of me hitting her in the face? Why were no photos taken for her so-called injuries?

The whole time in the back seat of the police car I was concerned about my dog the most. We then arrived at the police department, where my fingerprints were taken, and I was asked a few more questions. After my photo was taken, front and profile, I then was placed in a holding cell for 27 hours. It was the longest 27 hours of my entire life. The lights were overbearing and bright, and it was cold. There was a green mat that I laid on in the holding cell. Next to the mat was a toilet with a brick covering. I remember being so bored that I began counting how many bricks surrounded the room that I was in. There was also a payphone in the cell, and I made calls to Durabi and my birth mother because I knew that they would both answer the phone. I felt I could rely on them because whenever I contacted them, they answered.

Durabi was my biggest supporter in this case and really calmed my anxiety levels down. Dinner time was approaching, and it was time to eat. I was given several Hi-C juice boxes. I remember the flavors: Boppin' Strawberry and Flashin' Fruit Punch. I was also given the Banquet frozen dinner chicken nugget and french fries. It was better than what I thought I was going to be given. Five minutes felt like 45 minutes in that room, and there was no clock in sight.

The next day around 9:30 a.m., a man approached me and began asking me a few questions and then I was released from the holding cell and was given my advice of rights. My signature was required. As I was reading it, one of the police officers stated, "You can read it in the van, just sign it."

In my head, I was thinking *Don't you read before you sign things, ...idiot?* But I couldn't say that out loud. I listened and signed it and read it in the van as told. It was all so unreal to me because I was handcuffed with a cuffing belt on. The police officer then escorted me and another guy to the van, and we were driven to the court for arraignment. I was frightened because I didn't know what to expect. This was my second offense of domestic violence,

but in this case, I was innocent, and it was hearsay, and the evidence was against me because of an additional witness. I was praying for my freedom.

During this time, my faith was being tested. For the first time, I began praying obsessively. As we arrived at the court, we were put in another holding cell, which was even smaller than the one before. There was another inmate in the room with me, and I began talking to him and his situation was very similar to mine. My heart dropped as the door opened because I was so eager to get out. As the door opened, it was an OCJ (Oakland County Jail) prisoner. Not to be stereotypical or anything, but he looked like your standard prisoner. We all began to talk in the holding cell, and I wanted to know what he did to land him jail time because I felt like that was going to happen to me.

I remember looking at his jumpsuit, saying to myself *Ok, God, I understand I can't force the truth on other people, but please get me out of this. I didn't deserve this, nor did I do this. I know you know my heart.*

The door then opened again, and we were all handcuffed again with cuffs and a cuffing belt and escorted to court in a single filed line. As we entered the court room, the only person I knew in the court room was my birth mother. My palms were so sweaty as I waited for my case to be addressed. I could feel the saliva being swallowed down my throat. I could hear my heart pulsating.

When it was my time, I was told to stand and state my full name.

As I stood, I gave my name as well as background information about myself. I thought the judge would be lenient because I thought my background was decent for my age. I was hoping to be able to leave on a cheap personal bond.

As I waited on her decision, I remember looking at my birth mother and mouthing to her that "I was scared." She looked back and mouthed back, "I know."

Bail was set at $10,000 full amount not 10%, and my court date was two and a half weeks after, and Christmas was approaching. My heart dropped because I didn't have $10,000 nor did anybody I know. I was shaking because after the other people were arraigned, I was going to jail. I was able to get a phone call before I was taken to jail, and I called Durabi and my birth mother. They told me not to worry, and they would get me out. As I went back into the holding cell, I just wanted to cry and freak out. But I knew that my faith was being tested. I let a few tears out and kept praying to myself. One of the other inmates got the same consequence as me, and he was younger. He cried and cried, I asked him could I hug him and told him that he would get through it. I knew that God wasn't going to leave me hanging.

The police officer opened the door and said, "What the fuck?" I had to explain that I was comforting him, and the police officer said that I shouldn't do that. We all then were escorted to the police van and were processed to OCJ (Oakland County Jail).

When I arrived, I instantly got shit from the guards.

"Looks like someone forgot to make a stop at the children village," one said, like I could help being five-foot-five.

As I analyzed my surroundings, I noticed a lot of tough-looking people; they looked pretty rough and dirty. I was a germaphobe, and the area had me paranoid. I noticed there was a big room with at least 35 guys sharing a sleeping space with thin blankets as pillows.

I began thinking, *I can't sleep next to strangers in one room, unaware of their intentions.* I became fearful but remained faithful in trusting that I was about to be released. There were several cells with people in them, and other rooms served for people who were coming off or having withdrawals from drugs.

After paperwork was completed, I and the guy who I was processed with were escorted into a room and were asked if we had eaten, which we hadn't. They gave us both a brown paper bag with our lunches. Inside of the bag were two end pieces of bread, two pieces of bologna, two packets of mustard, two cookies and a lemon. Yes, a fucking lemon ... out of all fruits.

I put the food back into the bag and rolled it up, and thought, *I'm not eating that.* Another officer then escorted us to the area to get our inmate clothes. It freaked me out because I was looking at a guy in an OCJ suit, and next thing, I knew I was in one. They asked my size. I then moved to the strip search line. An officer told me to take all of my clothes off. Piece by piece.

"Remove your shirt.

"Remove your pants.

"Remove your socks.

"Remove your underwear.

"Spread your arms.

"Lift your balls.

"Turn around.

"Bend over.

"Spread your cheeks.

"Cough

"Put these clothes on.

"Breedlove, you're in and out."

I asked what that meant.

An officer said, "Someone posted your bond."

I overheard another officer say, "Seriously?"

I was even surprised. I was wondering how the hell Durabi and my birth mother came up with $10,000 to get me out. I was so happy I knew God wouldn't let me go down like that. Before I left, I told the boy who was processed with me that everything was going to be okay and to stay strong and that his bond would be posted, too. I was then taken to get my mug shot before I was taken to be discharged. As I was getting my photo taken, there were four guards in the photo room. They were assholes for no reason and were aware that I was leaving.

So, they really gave me shit.

"Ohhh, we have miss pretty princess here."

"Are you wearing your sister's jeans?"

I remember a guard asking me, "Do you talk?"

I shook my head.

He then said, "Oh, we don't process people who don't speak, what's your name?"

I said, "Christopher Breedlove."

"Oh, you do talk."

Another guard said, "We heard you were on top of another inmate. That's kind of weird, isn't it?"

After I was guided to another bench where I sat until my paperwork came back to sign. I changed clothes and returned the prisoner clothing.

Thirty-five minutes of jail was enough for me to realize that I never wanted to be in a situation where someone took me out of character for the slightest thing, and that if I was ever threatened to have the police called on me, I would be the first one to call.

I was then released and guided to the exit doors, and in a room on the outside was my birth mother and a bondsman. I was so happy to be out of there and to see a familiar face.

First thing I asked was "How did you come up with $10,000?"

My birth mother told me Durabi had the connection to the bondsman, and Durabi and my birth mother paid $500 each resulting in a 10% deposit of $1,000 on their end and the bondsman did the rest. I felt so loved by the both of them knowing that I at least had them in those moments when my mother was against me.

There was a series of papers I had to sign, and I had to ensure that I would be at court or my birth mother and Durabi would have been responsible for paying back $10,000.

Reflection Point

We all have different peak points, and once we overcome those peaks spiritually, we are given good things. What this entire situation taught me in looking back on things is to not give any person control over your emotions. Instead of reacting, learn to walk away from conflict. I am also learning to forgive my adoptive mother. Something I have learned to implement was from the advice of my birth father. He told me to be so kind to other people that they feel guilty and to stop reacting aggressively because nobody wants to be around an aggressive person. His words really stuck with and made me want to have more compassion for my mother, despite her reasonings for doing what she did.

Durabi's Patterned Return

Dear Breedlove,

Fast forward a few days after everything that happened with my family, I ended up going to see Durabi for the holidays because I was planning to move to Georgia to work on things with him for the second time. However, that was cut short because I had to return to Michigan for court. We made an agreement to create a solution on how to be together after being on and off for over five years. I was able to spend two weeks with him until I had to come back for court. The two weeks that I was able to spend with Durabi were the most peaceful two weeks that I have ever experienced.

Although they were the most peaceful, this did not mean they came without some drama. During my two-week stay with Durabi, we began to argue more the closer it got to my court date. We argued about old issues that were not solved and had a disagreement about finances. I felt extremely upset during those moments because I thought why bring up finances when I was unsure of my freedom and if I would be able to return to Georgia to start my life with him. I just wanted his support, which I received—just not enough during these moments.

I must admit that this fight was my fault and that was something that I do take accountability for because I was the instigator. I was hurting from the situation regarding my family, and I felt suicidal. During that fight with Durabi, I terrorized him for eight hours. I threatened myself over and over again, saying that I would kill myself. I completely lost control over myself and my emotions. I grabbed forks, knives, whatever I could to harm myself because I was such a mess inside. The intense disagreement with Durabi took me back to past moments where I felt suicidal, and I projected those feelings off on him unintentionally. Durabi tried his best to hide all objects from me to keep me safe. After he did that, since harming myself was a way of taking anger out on myself instead of harming others, I grew livid because Durabi was limiting me from hurting myself, and then I took my anger out on him and hurt him.

I didn't even realize how much suffering I was experiencing internally. Half of me couldn't believe that I was harming the one person I loved most, but the other half felt as if I was inflicting the pain he inflicted on me over the years, and I was emotionally releasing from every single person that ever hurt me, including him.

As I reflect on things while writing this book, I realize that in those moments with Durabi I was projecting my feelings of abandonment from my biological parents and adoptive parents onto him and became destructive to myself and him. Durabi kept his composure and didn't lay a finger on me; he helped pack my things and drove me to Atlanta to catch my flight for the next day. This all happened on New Year's. What a way to bring in New Year's, right? I started to realize that I hurt the person I loved the most and felt even more abandoned. As we drove, I tried to exit the car as the car was in motion. We then stopped at a gas station, in which I tried running into oncoming traffic on the freeway. I felt so low about myself, and I was unsure of how things were going to go with the court, especially it being my second domestic violence offense. I was afraid.

After Durabi dropped me off at the hotel with my dog and my belongings, I felt so hurt that I hurt him because I was hurting and the life that I wanted with my partner was gone. I started to feel intense resentment toward my adoptive mother. I thought if she hadn't lied about me punching her, none of this would have happened, and I would have been living with the one person I loved.

A part of me felt like my mom took that away from me, and I was very angry about that.

Reflection Point

During the course of my relationship with Durabi, I was obsessive, avoidant of my mental health and issues surrounding my adoption, and much more. Before entering a relationship, it is imperative to clear the internal guck and heal your inner child before trying to love another person. Durabi and I both struggled with that; however, we both had a strange way of forgiving each other during the worst of times, which is what drew me to him.

Another lesson that I learned from Durabi was to first "acknowledge your wrongdoings and hold yourself accountable opposed to explaining yourself. When you explain yourself when a person is sharing their feelings, it could be perceived as disregarding their emotions. After having parts of me emotionally disregarded for so long, I didn't know it would have an effect on dealing with people I loved. I unintentionally would explain myself and never acknowledge other people's emotions.

As I reflect on my relationship with Durabi, I know that it was essential in me seeking and finding myself. He was the first person to tell me what I needed to heal my abandonment issues and that he could not be everything that I needed (Dad, Mom, lover, friend). I didn't understand that until I realized I had a lot of issues. Durabi was a key connector in helping me gather the courage to find out who I was. He was always harsh with me, but I learned better when I had some fire under my feet. Durabi, too, is currently healing his toxic traits—like I am.

What my relationship with Durabi also taught me is that sometimes you meet people who are needed in your journey to get you to confront the ugly parts to who you are. Also, I learned the importance of focusing on the present.

| | | | | | | |

January 3

Dear Breedlove,

The day of my court hearing, I was full of anxiety and stress, and I really didn't know what to expect. I didn't hear much from my family for a matter of weeks, so it was going to be my first time seeing anybody. My birth mother and I went through the metal detector and sat outside the court room for a few hours; it was quite a lengthy process. I then saw my mother and father walking past. They didn't acknowledge me or my birth mother. My heart dropped as soon as I saw my other mother, and anger rose toward her because in the police report she stated that I hit her multiple times in the face. The court appointed lawyer came out after hours of waiting and documented my side of the story before proceeding into the courtroom for the hearing.

We then proceeded into the courtroom and waited until my case was called. When the case finally began, I had to basically testify as guilty because in the police report, I admitted to knocking my mother's phone out of her hand, which I did do. I was not going to lie over something that I did not do, and I just wanted to be honest about everything. I did not hit her, but I did knock her phone out of her hand. I was scared because I knew that I could not have any police contact because of my previous record with my father.

The judge then asked me some questions. I remember feeling annoyed because she had said that "I was ungrateful and that I should be grateful to have been chosen," which I was, but there were a lot of things that I did not agree with how my adopted family handled things in reference to the adoption. I did not tell her that because at that point I was just more so focused on my freedom. So, I explained myself and asked the lawyer could I get it reduced down to disorderly person, and that is exactly what happened. I got my case reduced from domestic violence to disorderly person and again because I admitted to knocking her phone out of her hand, it was considered damaging and touching my mother's property. I now have a misdemeanor case on my record due to me lacking emotional control.

As court dismissed, I remember seeing my family leaving. On the way out, my aunt left the courtroom and gave me a kiss on the cheek, I remember thinking to myself, *Bitch, why are you giving me a kiss?* I was still pissed off with her for hitting me with a laundry cart despite the fact I never laid hands on my mother. I also remember the saddened look on my mother's face; she looked in my eyes, and she just looked like she was so sorry, but I couldn't help to feel anger. This wasn't the first time my mom lied to people claiming that I laid hands on her and my sister.

The judge told me that I didn't belong in jail, and I clearly felt the same because one of my biggest fears was getting gang raped in jail. I felt elated that I didn't have to go to jail. However, I was still hurting because my parents didn't want to address the adoption at all because of their own insecurities. I didn't really know how to feel about any of it. It was difficult to process. I was aware that I was in the wrong for disrespecting my mother, but it also took two to tango.

| | | | | | | |

Switch Up

Dear Breedlove,

I felt confused and angry, wondering how I got to the point of being where I was. My birth mother and I drove back to her home and decompressed for the day. The next day, I called the police and scheduled an officer to get my belongings from my adoptive mother. It saddened me that things like this were happening.

When we arrived at my mom's place, I told my birth mother to park on the street before my mother arrived because I wanted to be safe. I didn't want to violate any restrictions that were given by the court. I felt as if my mom could lie and say I hit her; I didn't want to see what more damage she could do because I didn't trust her anymore. A police car had passed by twice, and I got the signal to come over, and I walked to my mother's house. My dad then answered the door. I proceeded to pack some of my things and get everything in my birth mother's car. At the time, my sister stayed in my adoptive parents' home. Throughout the process of going in and out retrieving my things, my sister didn't come outside.

My parents didn't want her to come outside "for some reason." My father helped me break down my dog's crate.

It was kind of an awkward feeling to have my dad helping me pack up all my belongings from where I was raised through my teenage years to going into my birth mother's car. My adoptive father didn't say anything to my birth mother. He just helped me pack my belongings, and they told my sister to stay inside. I guess, looking back on things, I wish that they were more open about allowing my sister to meet our birth mother because it could have benefited her and her healing process; however, they didn't want that.

I felt like they were only thinking about themselves in the situation. One minute I was with my family, and then almost a year later, I had nowhere to go. I quit my job, and I ended up having to live with my birth mother. When we got back to her house, I felt angry because I didn't want to live with her, and I was upset!

You're probably wondering where my birth father was during this time. I briefly shared some of the story with him when things calmed down. At that time, I was dealing with my own insecurities. I began to want approval from my birth parents. I felt like I had to hold myself to a higher standard with my birth father, and I was embarrassed and ashamed by everything that happened with my adoptive mother, so I didn't tell him about everything until court was complete.

| | | | | | |

Living & Working with My Birth Mom

Dear Breedlove,

As I left court with my birth mother, her home was my new home for the time being. I remember settling myself and my dog in getting accustomed to everything. At the time it was a lot to process. Going from just meeting her to now living with her. I felt that I was forced into the situation.

I spent most days for almost two months sitting in my room and sleeping. I was mostly angry because I didn't see myself at the point that I was. It was confusing for me because I was still processing and accepting that both of my birth parents were in my life. I was still struggling with guilt from my adoptive family. It was overwhelming for me because I felt the need to meet expectations that were unspoken of from my birth mother. Sometimes, I really enjoyed being around her, especially when she was happy. I liked seeing her chipper. However, there were times when I felt like disengaging with her because she was pessimistic, complaining a lot, and I didn't like her use of excessive swearing. It bothered me because I wanted to respect her, but those things made it harder for me to do so. Not to compare, but my other parents never showed me their weakness, or they rarely complained about their own issues. It was even rare to hear them swear. I do believe there is a difference in sharing issues opposed to complaining about them.

Aside from an emotional experience, this situation taught me a lot about myself and my birth mother. I began to notice how passive she was and how she internalized all of her guilt and pain. I also learned that she too was resilient. She had a tough life and worked a lot to distract herself from thinking, even though she hated her job. I even noticed how hard she was on herself and how giving she was to others. She put others before herself every time. During my time with her, she took care of an old man named John who also lived there. She would prepare his food, bathe him, handle doctor appointments, everything. She was so generous and would refuse help from others. Seeing her take care of John every day allowed me to see how compassionate she was and who she truly was aside from her past. She was the same way with me. I struggled getting a job due to having "disorderly person (violent)" on my record. She helped me a lot financially, allowing me to save and pursue my freelance work more. Throughout the process of my probationary period, she took me to every appointment I had and allowed me the freedom to use her car because mine was repossessed the year I met her. I noticed I began to gravitate to her more, and my guard slowly began to come down toward her. I began to be more open and receptive in understanding her and learning to love her. She was a great support system for listening to me ramble all the time, and she would listen attentively. She listened to my dreams and aspirations and had an extreme eagerness in understanding and knowing who I was. Living with my birth mother taught me to be more humble and to emotionally understand other people's journey and struggles.

One of the turning points aside from living with my

birth mother came from me working at the same job with her for a little less than a month. I needed a source of income because I quit my job prior to all the court stuff happening because I had the intentions of moving. I couldn't leave the state because of the incident that occurred with my adoptive mother. I literally hated the job that I worked with my birth mother, and I honestly couldn't comprehend how she did the same job for over nine years. The job was tedious; it was manufacturing work, and I hated it. Waking up at 4 a.m., being at work for 6 a.m., and getting off at 3:30 every single day. I felt drained. I only worked with my birth mother for about three weeks, and then I quit. I could not handle it; it was not for me, and it was not purposeful.

Reflection Point

Whenever I felt like jobs were not purposeful, or I was not implementing the skills that I had, or I didn't like the people, I just quit; I never really had a consistent job history. However, I will say that during the time of working with my birth mother, I was able to see how she was outside of home life and how other people viewed her. She was just a very sweet, giving person who made herself suffer from her mistakes.

| | | | | | | |

Papers

Dear Breedlove,

After processing the sequence of events that occurred over the first few months, I kept having ongoing thoughts of revisiting my adoption papers.

I was in foster care for 10 months, and in the papers, it stated that I was fearful of a man in one of the foster care homes I was in. The characteristics were very brief; they said that the foster father was a drunk and went out all the time and that I was fearful of him. It made me think maybe I was fearful because something happened to me, and perhaps that's where my anger stemmed from before I was adopted.

Reflection Point

As I dove deeper into my adoption papers and started to analyze my story, I started thinking perhaps my anger developed from my close relationships constantly being taken away from me. It started off with my birth mother (primal wound). I was with her, then taken to a foster care home for 10 months, then placed into another foster home for two years, and then finally adopted by my current family.

Dr. Phil

Dear Breedlove,

I've always had a really big issue with people ignoring my messages or phone calls, especially my parents, and I began calling them obsessively.

I remember having feelings of trying to shift my energy. I wanted to see what I could draw into my life if I tried to focus more on the positives. One day when I was running on the treadmill at the gym, *Dr. Phil* was on the television. I never noticed the TVs until day. What caught my attention were the following words on the screen: "Tell us your story today."

As soon as I went home, I applied for the show, sharing my adoption story. The very next day, the executive producer contacted me. They were actually interested in my story. However, in order to get approved for the show, all parties had to agree. My birth parents agreed; however, my adoptive family of course did not. I couldn't understand the big deal in talking about adoption and how great my sister and I turned out. It's almost as if my adoptive family viewed talking about it as a bad thing.

When my adoptive parents said no, I remember thinking to myself this could have benefit all of us and bring awareness to issues regarding adoption. I also wanted to use that opportunity to market my book to help gain profit for myself and my family and to impact others. But they were limited

in their perspective because they were insecure about their involvement in the story, but I digress.

During the phone conversation with my adoptive parents, aside from asking about being on *Dr. Phil*, I told my father that I needed an apology to heal. My adoptive father then replied that he wasn't apologizing for anything and that I was an ungrateful kid, I was selfish, and I didn't know how to make any sacrifices like he did. I was offended by his comment because it made me feel like an item. I understood people say things in the heat of the moment, but what I believe is that when people say things when they are angry, odds are they did mean it, they just didn't mean to say it in that particular moment.

My adoptive father and I both began to get upset, and he then hung up on me mid-sentence. I called back and asked him could he try to understand my perspective. My dad then told me that the way I was acting was making him regret adopting me. In those moments, my heart shattered, and I told him "f*** you" about three times. I understood that he was upset, but I also felt like he was the parent and should have held himself accountable. If a child needed something for healing, dammit, you give it to them.

It was so easy for me to forgive, but I could never forget. I used to write my parents letters, apologizing for what I did when I was younger, and I couldn't even get an apology from my parents in those moments. I then called my mother and said the same things to her, and she told me to leave them alone. How I viewed her response was that nobody wanted to be held accountable to the things that they said. I began blocking all of my family members, their phone numbers, social media…everything. I felt like they genuinely did not understand where I was coming from nor were they trying to.

Reflection Point

It hurt me to know that I had to learn how to move on and not get an apology from the very people who raised me. In some ways, they were in denial of their own guilt. In those moments of the conversation, I realized it was best for me to separate myself from my family until they maybe one day understood how to have a regard for my emotions and put their emotions aside to address the reality of the truth. Yes, the truth hurts, but the truth also heals, and I was in a place of working on healing myself, and I hoped my family decided to heal themselves and to continue to move forward.

In trying to distance myself from my adoptive family, I thought maybe people gave apologies in different ways, rather it be pretending like nothing happened or making humor of the situation. Even with this awareness of people possibly apologizing in different ways, I'm too much of a cynic to accept that.

There were a lot of misconceptions with how my parents thought that I felt about my adoption. In my eyes, I felt I was emotionally mature enough and open to learning duality and accepting both parts of me in an effort to heal my scars and wounds internally.

One of my friends had said something that was so profound about their own adoption story: "The term ungrateful is a term that people use when they feel threatened by someone who didn't turn out the way that they imagined. When I began questioning my past and their motives, my parents got defensive and fell back and said that I was ungrateful because they didn't expect me to question anything."

I believed my adoptive parents felt so arrogant about them providing us with such a good life that when I began to question the adoption, issues arose because I questioned my role in the family. My questioning put a dent in their reality of what our family really was.

Another lesson I learned regarding the disagreement with my adoptive father was "age does not mean you are evolved." Our parents and our elders progress and evolve at different levels mentally and spiritually and deserve a space to do so. I realized my ability in the situation with my adoptive and birth family was that I was aware of everyone's perspective in the situation, and I wanted my family to understand *my* perspective.

Reflection Point II

As I reflected on this part of my life, I realized that I was extremely prideful in focusing on what I wanted emotionally without trying to fully understand where my family was at on their journey. Who was I to force them to apologize because I felt hurt?

Alternative View

I think that my parents felt threatened by me finding my birth family and acted in ways that expressed fear. Even though they said they were not hurt, they actually were and did not know how to communicate those feelings. Looking back on things, I could have done a better job at cradling their feelings as opposed to thinking that my emotions mattered more than theirs. Throughout the process of bonding with my birth parents, my adoptive parents felt like I was trying to replace them. I couldn't understand why I couldn't love everybody. My goal wasn't to replace them but to understand all parts of who I was. They cannot be replaced. Nor can my birth parents who created me. Both of my families were essential in building my character, experiences, and personality. All of them were a part of me.

| | | | | | |

Genetics

Dear Breedlove,

In the beginning of building my relationships with my birth parents, I called them by their first names, Undrey and Brenda. I remember vividly telling the both of them that I would never call them Mom or Dad. There were multiple instances in which my birth mother would get upset at me calling her by her first name or not really calling her anything.

One night in particular, she said that she felt like she was being used and that I was not genuine. I told her that her doing something for me for three months was not worth her getting the title of being my mother when she was absent for the past 21 years. I felt really bad saying that at first, but a part of me actually meant that. I recall breaking down crying, asking, "Is that what you want, for me to call you Mom? Mom, Mom, Mom, Mom, Mom, is that what you want?"

Of course, I was being sarcastic, but as I was saying it, I began to experience an overflow of emotions that I didn't know were there.

We both started crying; in that moment, it was freeing to accept that she did give birth to me, and she deserved to be acknowledged in some way.

Reflection Point

A lot of times, people think that you only can have room in your heart just to love the people who raised you, especially in cases of adoption. To me, I had enough room in my heart to love every single person involved in my story because without any of them, I wouldn't even exist. Again that leads me to my point of humans are not objects, and we don't have ownership over anyone or anything, not to mention we don't have ownership over our own souls. Who are we to think that we are limited to loving only a few people? Love is universal and the most powerful of emotions, and we all deserve it. Another perspective I look at in regard to my adoption story is that my biological parents deserve spiritual closure, too, and they deserve healing as did I in understanding who I was and where I came from. I felt I was brought back into my birth family's life to repair and heal them and their past scars, too. I found myself in awe sometimes of my story. Fluctuating between acceptance and disbelief. I was so intrigued with my birth parents I would often glare at their images and study their characteristics searching for myself in them.

| | | | | | |

Healing Anger with Birth Dad

Dear Breedlove,

My birth father and I had a very playful relationship. I felt like a kid again with him. We would wrestle, crack jokes on each other, talk for hours about spirituality and complex things. I loved how he was persistent in finding ways to bond with me, listen to me, and be a part of my life. I love him for that. One day, I went to his house; he lived 15 minutes away from my birth mother. Every Wednesday, we spent time together. On this Wednesday, we were wrestling, and things got really serious. My birth father asked me to stop, and for some reason, I couldn't stop showing feelings of aggression toward him during our wrestling encounter. A part of me felt triggered, and I didn't even realize that I had repressed anger toward my birth father.

He told me to sit down, and we didn't talk for about 30 minutes.

After the half-hour of silence, he asked me, "Where did that aggression come from? You know, I have struggle with aggression issues, too, and I had to put that part of my life behind me."

I shared with him that I struggled from anger issues and that I was angry with him, but I didn't want to be mad at him.

I told him I was mad at him for not being there. I was mad at him for not seeing me be born, I was mad that it took him three years to see if I was his child. I was so angry with him, and I didn't even know where these feelings were coming from.

I broke down crying. Who knew that moment would be one of the most pivotal moments of my life? Instead of him calling the police or having me arrested or saying mean things to me or disregarding my emotions, my birth father addressed his wrongdoings and apologized as he always did. My birth father was a solid figure to me, and I wanted to be like him. He motivated me to dive into building a stronger relationship with God in addition to motivating me to remain abstinent. I really valued my relationship with him.

My birth parents had a way of constantly reassuring me and reminding me that they were sorry. Every now and again, my birth father would call me some days and would break down apologizing for his absence. I felt both of my birth parents sincerely were sorry for how things happened with me and that they also loved me. I felt it in my heart, and I loved them, too.

I learned that people make mistakes, and nobody deserves to suffer from their mistakes … nobody. My birth father and I chose to move forward and to not look back at the past and focus on our relationship right now. I remember he said, "I love you, son, and I'm sorry," and I told him, "I love you, too, Dad," and that was my first time calling him Dad. For the longest, I chose to call my birth father Pops because I was avoiding acknowledging him. Prior to that, I called him by his first name as well. The moment I called him Dad was so freeing because I was able to acknowledge him as the man who created me.

Not to mention for the first time, somebody in my life eased and comforted me in my intensely emotional state. I was able to calm myself down, and my birth father calmed me down, and it was a very healing experience for me.

In addition to everything with my birth father, there was another moving point in which I saw how much he cared about me. I shared some of my insecurities with him, telling him how could he love me as much as he loved my other siblings when he saw all of them be born, but he didn't see me, that really hurt me. He told me that I was of him, and he loved me just as much as my siblings, and it made my heart full hearing that. It also made my heart full knowing that my siblings accepted me and that they loved me. For a while I struggled with feelings of thinking that I was imposing on their lives or our father, and they all affirmed me that I was not and that I too had the same rights because we were of the same DNA. I cherish my birth siblings so much because aside from them being my siblings, they were becoming my friends.

Confidence

Dear Breedlove,

So roughly over the entire year of 2018, I was more focused on building relationships with my birth family since I really couldn't have much interaction with my adoptive mother and my adoptive family. I didn't have much contact with my adoptive family for almost the entire year. What I realized was that I was happy in building relationships with my birth family and was learning how to push my anger aside to understand them. It also helped that my birth parents communicated in the same ways as I did. There was an unspoken mutual emotional understanding with both of my birth parents and my siblings. I felt like a part of me was complete. Before finding my birth family, I lacked a lot of confidence in myself and my abilities, and I had a lot of issues that I really couldn't figure out where they were coming from nor why. As I got to know my birth family and continue to learn about them, I realized a lot of things sometimes could be from generational curses. It is up to us to listen to our parents to avoid partaking in the same mistakes that they have.

I also noticed that some of my birth parents' experiences were almost identical to some of my experiences. It was so important for me to understand who they were and how they got to their life so that I could make the changes necessary to avoid making the same mistakes that they did. Having my birth parents in my life restored a part of me that died.

For years, I wondered who I was, and I was fortunate enough in having healthy relationships with both my birth parents. Yes, I was raised by my adoptive parents, and they did a phenomenal job. On a spiritual level, I am Undrey, and I am Brenda. I was the union of both of them, and it was so healing for me to finally accept my past and for the first time in my life be okay with it and to let go of what other people thought or if they thought me seeking my past was a selfish act. I let go of all guilt and accepted who I was and where I came from.

| | | | | | | |

Perspective

Dear Breedlove,

A lot of times, what I noticed regarding adoption is often the adoptee feels guilty about building relationships with their birth family out of consideration for their adoptive family's feelings. I personally feel like adoptive families should be firm and comfortable in their relationship with their child and be more open in discussing the adoption. If the adoption is transparent, and the adoptee has a supportive healthy and safe environment, finding out about their past and making sense of their lives should easily be done in the open and not in secrecy.

Something that I one day hope to do is have a Christmas dinner with my birth family and my adoptive family all together in a lovely union. That would make me so happy. However, even if I never get that, I'm already happy discovering my story and my truth and discovering who I am.

Alternative Perspective

I also wanted to be in a place of understanding. For example, I wanted to be understanding of my birth parents' mind frame and the struggles that they went through and to learn to forgive them. They, too, are human and make mistakes. If you are an adoptee reading this, something that I challenge you to do is to put yourself in your birth-parent's shoes and try to understand their perspective as opposed to just being hateful or vengeful toward them because they abandoned you or gave you up or whatever the situation may be. Perhaps the story was meant to be written that way.

|| || || ||

Mistakes

Dear Breedlove,

I learned through both my birth mother and father that my birth mother was married to my older sister's father, and he would abuse her often. He was a drunk and also the reason in which my birth mother lost another baby because he threw her down the stairs. My birth mother didn't know what to do when she was trapped. All those things, in addition to losing her parents, led her to use drugs and cheat on her husband with my birth father.

As the first year of knowing my birth mother progressed, I was able to get to know her more, and I could feel her pain. I could feel her sorrow, and I didn't want to be another reason or thing to add to her pain or sorrow. I wanted to make her happy and to add to her happiness because I felt her sadness, and I felt her sincere apology. I knew that she loved me. She made a mistake in which she acknowledged numerous times. Despite the fact she was out of my life for 21 years, I let my guard down in the efforts of showing her that I cared about her, too.

Who knew that she would be there for me the way she has been over the course of our reunion, in addition to being a healing component to my soul?

Reflection Point

In retrospect, I had zero expectations that any of this would ever happen. I also realized that whenever the mind or soul really wants something, and you seek it aggressively, it will manifest.

When I learned to look at my life through my birth mother's lens, I learned to understand her perspective and why she did what she did because if I was her, I would have done the same thing. I think to myself, *What would I have done if it was me getting beat, and both of my parents passed away, and I struggling to provide for my children? How would I feel?* I am now at a place, feeling as if I was placed in my birth mother's life to help her gain a backbone because she was such a passive person, and she felt guilty for all of her wrongdoings, and she couldn't tell people no. I noticed that there were so many people in her life who claimed that they loved her but just drained her or took away from her or used her. I didn't like it; it made me angry to see that. I felt as if God placed me back in her life to show her that it was okay to say no and to not feel guilty about her past mistakes. I wanted to show her that she deserved love and, a new beginning of life as opposed to making herself suffer, and forgiveness of self.

Even as she reads this book, I hope that she is learning to forgive herself because she's been through so much, and she deserves healing and peace, and I am so grateful that she chose to carry and deliver me instead of abort me because she did have that option, and she didn't. I also viewed my reunion with my birth mother as a major blessing to my birth mother. My birth mother gave birth to multiple children in which three lived, including myself. She never got a chance to mother any of her children, and I feel that my presence in my birth mother's life was for her to feel like a mother, being there for me in any way she could.

In regard to my birth father, I felt the same way about him; he didn't deserve to suffer for his wrongdoings. Yes, he made mistakes; yes, he wasn't there, but in the almost two years of me being in reunion with him, he had made it his responsibility to be there whenever I needed him. He would call me almost every other day to check on me. During our initial stage of reconnecting, I had purchased a car, and there were a lot of things wrong with the car. Anytime I needed something with the car, he came over to fix it and to help me with it and to show me what to do if something else happened.

I'd never experienced that before. We would play video games together for hours and talk and bonded nicely. Not that my adoptive parents did anything wrong, but I felt like our love languages were different. My birth parents knew how to love me without me directing them on how to do it. I was privileged to bond with both of my birth parents, and it made me question who I was because I felt like I was beginning to become a new person; it even made me reevaluate my sexuality and thoughts of redefining my relationship with God.

Reflection Point

Growing up, my adoptive mother was overbearing, and my adoptive father was submissive; the roles were significantly reversed with my birth parents.

My adoptive father never really hugged or kissed me or told me he loved me that much, and that's because he wasn't raised like that, which I understood. For the past two years, my birth father has shown me the love that I needed from a masculine figure. He would tell me that he loved me and remained transparent about his feelings toward me and how he was happy to have me in his life. The same thing with my birth mother; she was a really great listener, and even if she didn't like what I was talking about, she would listen to my emotions and regard them.

In my eyes, I felt it was important to bond with my birth parents because I knew I was healing two other people while healing myself. There was a silent natural connection with both of them.

Reflection Point II

Even now as I write these last few words of this book, I realize we are all on different schedules to grow. We don't grow at the same time as other people internally or spiritually. I felt my birth parents were on the path seeking to heal, but the family that raised me was not on that same path, and it was not my job to force them to do so. As I reflect throughout the process of completing this book, I realize that in some ways I was aggressive in forcing the truth on my family that raised me, and it caused a lot of friction. I began asking myself questions such as: how is my pride helping me right now? Who am I to be a judge of the progress of another person's journey?

Sometimes, we forget our parents are people, too, and they have their own inner child and experiences to heal. They are not JUST our parents. What I find the most rewarding about this whole experience in solving my past mystery is that in getting to know my birth family, I have grown to have a greater love for my family that raised me. I am also learning not to reject love or be overly critical of how I am being loved because people love differently. Sometimes we want people to love us a certain way, but perhaps they can only love in the only way they know how or perhaps it's all that they can offer.

Wait, It's Not Over?

Dear Breedlove,

As I finished up this book, I honestly thought that my story was over, but it was not. There was more. I decided to revisit my adoption papers from the Central Adoption Registry again. I couldn't help but notice that I was in two foster care homes instead of one. I was determined to find the foster care home that was listed because only one of them were listed. I began doing some research, and I found the names of the first foster care home, which was the Smith family. I began doing copious amounts of research, and I located a few addresses of where they previously used to live.

I took it upon myself to drive to all the locations, so I spent at least three hours driving to multiple locations with the papers that I had, and I kept running into dead ends. All the houses that I drove to were either abandoned or the wrong address.

The first house that I went to a man followed me around, saying that the house was tore down; he was asking why I was looking, and I told him. He told me that I should let the past be the past and stop looking. At first, I almost listened to him. However, I've always been the type of person who wanted to dig and figure out things for myself and not listen to anybody.

After hours of driving and running into dead ends, I took it upon myself to research further. I paid at least $50 for background checks on finding the Smiths, and I ran into more addresses and tons of phone numbers. I contacted every single phone number, but none of the phone numbers worked. I began to get extremely frustrated, and I felt that maybe I should give up. Something in me just could not do that thought. I wanted to piece everything together and solve my life mystery. I desired to give myself answers, despite the fact I found my birth family and got the answers I needed from them. I still felt like something was missing.

I began pinpointing relatives on the background checks and found their information and where they lived. The first relative that came to mind to call was Beth. She was the first one I called with a working phone number, and I was excited when the phone rang, and a woman answered.

She asked, "Who is this?"

I told her my name was Christopher and that I was in a

foster care home with the Smiths, and I wanted more information.

She asked me how I got her contact information. I was honest and told her, "I did several background checks, and I was trying to locate the Smiths."

"What's your last name?"

"Diehr." I was still protecting my current identity.

She gasped, and I knew the name meant something to her.

"You used to call me TT," she said before telling me that she and the Smiths were saddened when I was removed from their home because they too wanted to adopt me.

Beth added that she would pass my information on to the Smith family and that they would call me within five minutes. I didn't think that they would call as fast as they did, but they called me within about 10 minutes of me hanging up the phone with Beth. The Smiths and I then scheduled a meet and greet at Beth's home a few days later.

Of course, I went alone.

So as the days went by, on that Wednesday, it was time for me to meet my foster family after 23 years. I was nervous and scared because I didn't know what to expect nor how to prepare myself for what to believe because it was proven that my adoption papers in the past had some false information. I wasn't sure if they would provide me with the truth or more false information.

As I got there, I remember entering their home, and as

soon as I entered, they said, "Oh wow, Chris, you look the exact same in the face. You haven't changed a bit, but you just have a little bit of hair on your face."

I started laughing, and I remember feeling confused by people that I didn't know telling me things I used to say and do as a child, but I had no recollection of what they were saying or a way of affirming their statements. It was mind blowing to grow up only seeing myself as 4 years old and up. When meeting my birth mother, my older sister had my one and only baby picture, so I never got the chance to see myself as a toddler.

My previous foster family had an entire photo album of me along with the other children I was in foster care with. It was so wild to see me in that light and see young pictures of me. I felt like in those moments I solved the beginning years of my life, and I was able to finally see what happened and piece everything together. I was overwhelmed with so many emotions, and I remember feeling and thinking to myself, "Oh my God, I was so cute." Not that the cuteness subsided or anything, but I just was so cute, and I couldn't stop staring at myself. I literally remember thinking to myself, *Oh my God, that's me*, like I literally could not believe that's me.

In addition to looking at the photos, they addressed why I was removed, and they couldn't adopt me, and they were supposedly really upset about it. They said that I put up a fight because I didn't want to leave. It was difficult for me to not believe what they were saying because in the images that they showed me, I was smiling, and I looked somewhat happy. They then shared that as a child, I had a lot of anger issues, and that was eye-opening for me to see because even as an adult I had a lot of anger issues from not healing my primal wound and feelings of abandonment and rejection.

During my time visiting my first foster care family, I was able to put together the timelines and understand some things that I didn't before even the brief memory that I shared with you that I had prior to being adopted. The memory was two men arguing and one guy had a gap in his tooth and a short lady always was in the kitchen with a Bob hairstyle. Turns out the short lady with the Bob hairstyle was Mrs. Smith, and the guy with the Apple hat and the gap tooth was one of their relatives whose name was Boo. It was so amazing to me to actually understand some of the memories that I had even though I was still confused by some things. I just viewed that maybe it wasn't my job to know every little detail but for the most part, I solved my life mystery, and I finally knew who I was after 25 years.

Reflection Point

What this last experience taught me was to always trust your instincts or motive in desiring something. A deep desire that I wanted was to heal my past so that it could stop impacting my future and close relationships.

Closing

Dear Breedlove,

Throughout the process of my story, I have learned to accept all people involved in my story as they are—despite the fact some days are harder than others due to me having to live my life separate with my adoptive and birth family. The most important lessons that my life experiences have led me to as I close is the importance of taking your mental health seriously and addressing your childhood traumas. For years, I repressed what I was dealing with mentally, and in some way thought I was in denial about my mental health because I felt unheard. But I soon reached a point in which I admitted to myself that there could be some issues mentally, I began intensive therapy, EMDR, hypnotherapy, and visited a psychiatrist and was evaluated for a few months. After roughly a year, I was diagnosed with PTSD, Bi-polar Disorder and ADHD.

For the longest, I felt having a mental illness was a bad thing and that I was a bad person for having a mental illness. Sometimes, I even found myself ashamed to admit that I was dealing with anything because I didn't want people to say I was crazy, or I needed to be in a "looney bin." I was too arrogant to realize that I was flawed and my life experiences had humbled me and made me realize that I am very flawed.

Reflection Point

Within my millennial generation, I notice so many people in my age bracket and even younger suffer from mental illness and live in false realities due to social media. Struggling with feelings of not feeling good enough, not pretty enough, not smart enough. I feel as if our generation is becoming obsessed with superficial appearances, materials, and beauty, when in reality, none of those things matter. Something I thought about was what if social media was eliminated? Who would I be aside from my "online profiles"? What have I done to positively impact the community? Who am I? Do I know myself? Ask yourself the same things, and you may view social media differently. Of course, like everything else, it has its pros and cons. Take care of yourself mentally and never be afraid to seek help. Therapy and other methods dealing with healing mental illness have a lot of negative connotations to it. Don't allow others to make you feel guilty for becoming leveled. Not to mention your business does not leave your therapy session. In close, I hope that my shared story motivates you to seek your truth, face it, and acknowledge it in an effort to reach mental wellness.

You're probably waiting for an end to this story or some profound conclusion. Not in this book because I have found myself, and my story is still unfolding.

"Choose my instruction instead of silver, knowledge rather than choice gold, for wisdom is more precious than rubies, and nothing you desire can compare with her." -Proverbs 8:10-12

Lessons:

Lesson #1: Nobody deserves to suffer from their mistakes. Try to think of their experience and understand their perspective and the picture as a whole instead of your own "limited" perspective.

Lesson #2: Do not allow pride to hinder your relationships because you want to be right or prove a point.

Lesson #3: All of the negative things or challenges you endure are building character, and it's not the end of the world.

Lesson #4: Money is important. Being clear and healthy mentally is even MORE important.

Lesson #5: Do not allow other people to take you out of character due to you being triggered emotionally. (At least in my case certain things I was sensitive about because I was being triggered emotionally by a past memory, etc.). KNOW YOUR TRIGGERS and think of remedies to gain control over your triggers and how you manage the emotions that come with them.

Lesson #6: All riches are not financially based. Be rich in self-awareness, self-care, self-healing, and self-understanding.

Lesson #7: Do not force the truth on other people, allow space for them to accept the truth.

Lesson #8: Stop promising yourself un-promised time.

Lesson #9: Heal your inner child, primal wound, heal your past so you can be fully focused on the present.

Lesson #10: Get to the root of your anger, and or pain. Seek a therapist to see at least once a week. Therapy is extremely healthy and necessary to mentally thrive.

Lesson #11: Seek a lasting relationship with God and realize that he is the center of all positive things and creation.

Lesson #12: Don't explain yourself or your actions; acknowledge your wrongdoings and move forward.

Lesson #13: Don't listen to other people; figure things out relating to your journey on your own.

Lesson #14: When listening to other people, don't listen to defend yourself or what you are going to say next; listen actively.

Lesson #15: Be kind to others, even when they do not deserve it.

Lesson #16: Put your own puzzle pieces together; it is nobody else's job except yours.

Lesson #17: Don't put your happiness into other people because man will disappoint you every time. Put your happiness into God and finding out who you are.

Lesson #18: Stop blaming and shaming and take accountability.

Lesson #19: Be mindful of the company you keep, and think of why certain people are attracted into your life and what decisions good or bad are you making to allow certain people to enter your life.

Lesson #20: Being forceful in asking for an apology does NOT work.

Other Writings by Christopher Breedlove

I decided to share two of my writing pieces to stimulate your mind and make you question some things.

CLARITY

Clarity Clarity, why are you hard to find?

Opinions and visions overflowing my mind.

Which direction do I go? Or what decision do I make?

Terrified to make haste and let everything go to waste.

How do I become clean when I am not near?

Nor can I hear my own voice.

In the confusion of what others want me to be or project me to be...

How can I be sure of me? When all the thoughts I hear are potential possibilities, social disabilities, and versatilities? How does one quiet the mind? When everything is not aligned?

Clarity Clarity, internally I seek

Because deep down inside I am meek.

Clarity is something that is sought not given.

Clarity can be defined as taboo or forbidden...

Disengage from other people's view

So that you can personally get to know you.

Window Pain

I sat there staring out the window thinking what happened

I found myself blaming myself and then blaming you

my mind was racing, and I was feeling blue

Not to mention I wasn't supposed to be feeling you

Things with you just happened

And the timing felt right

And your light shined so bright

I felt drawn to you like a moth to a flame

I always envisioned you in my frame

with my last name

Despite the fact that life had different plans for us

teaching each other how to grow was a must

The fights we had were full of passion

but the only thing you were focused on was cashing

Even if that meant being unhappy with another person for
money

why did you leave for money when I was supposed to be your
honey?

You say love doesn't pay the bills

but money isn't there when you're the one that's ill

How could you be ok with settling for convenience?

Instead of building with me and building agreements

They say when things get hard you leave

but why leave me for someone when I was the one watering your seeds

Passion and spiritual connection are needed for a relationship to thrive

but you were only focused on being with someone to survive

As I look out the window and reflect

I was accustomed to your neglect

and now I respect

Your role to push me to my greatest change

and the written tattoo that I see every day of your name

and I'm reminded that it wasn't in vain.

Thank You

Dear Breedlove,

If you have made is this far, I appreciate you so much for reading my entire life story, and although some details are left out, I didn't necessarily want to make this book just about me. Seek answers fearlessly, and once you solve your past, you then can move forward.

"Before his downfall a man's heart is proud, humility comes before honor." -Proverbs 17:12

Much Love,

Christopher Anthony Lyndon Diehr Breedlove

Maven Gershom 0429

About the Author

My birth name was formerly Christopher Anthony Diehr; I now go by the name of Christopher L. Breedlove, which is now my legal name. I was born and raised in Southfield, MI, for the majority of my life. I was fortunate enough to have both of my parents as I was raised in a joint parenting household. I grew up middle class and had many educational resources.

At the age of 19, I graduated with my high school diploma and associate degree simultaneously from a dual enrollment program called Oakland Early College. After, I completed my undergrad degree in psychology from Central Michigan University. Currently, I am a graduate student, finishing my last remaining courses to attain my master's degree.

Aside from educational pursuits, I am a social media manager. I have experience running people's Facebook, Instagram, and Twitter accounts. A few of my clients have been seen on shows, such as *The Voice* and ABC's hit show *Duets*. I most recently dove into managing social media for local political clients.

Aside from marketing other people, I am a freelance model with over 13,000 Instagram followers (not that followers mean anything). I am currently signed with a placement agency based in Detroit, MI. I have booked several local commercials, and I am constantly expanding my print work.

In addition to my modeling endeavors, a colleague and I are currently working on a nonprofit catered to adoptees and children in the foster care system. The nonprofit that is still being developed is called Discover Your Truth. The goal of the nonprofit is to act as a voice for adoptees and kids in foster care and to focus on clearing stigmas regarding adoption and being a support system for children in the adoption community.

The primary goal and objective of my book is to share my life experience with anyone reading and to share some lessons and tips that I have learned throughout my journey. We all can learn something from each other's story. I hope you enjoyed.

"A good name is more desirable than great riches; to be esteemed is better than silver or gold." Proverbs 22:1

Our generation and social media sometimes make it look like everything is perfect in one's life. My story is to remind others that everything is not what it seems on the outside or online.

From a social media perspective, people always assumed that my 13,000-plus followers on Instagram meant that I was thriving or that my life was better than what it actually was. Or just because I took amazing photographs that I was "larger than life." But little did people know I was having my own battles just like everybody else.

We all have our own voice and our own story, and they all matter. This story was/is mine.

Made in the USA
Columbia, SC
27 July 2020